Wayland Hoyt

Along the Pilgrimage

Wayland Hoyt

Along the Pilgrimage

ISBN/EAN: 9783337293932

Printed in Europe, USA, Canada, Australia, Japan

Cover: Foto ©Lupo / pixelio.de

More available books at **www.hansebooks.com**

ALONG THE PILGRIMAGE.

WAYLAND HOYT, D. D.,

AUTHOR OF "HINTS AND HELPS FOR THE CHRISTIAN LIFE," "PRESENT LESSONS FROM DISTANT DAYS," "GLEAMS FROM PAUL'S PRISON."

PHILADELPHIA :
AMERICAN BAPTIST PUBLICATION SOCIETY,
1420 Chestnut Street.

PREFACE.

For the half-hours, the bits of leisure along the pilgrimage, this little book is meant. If for any pilgrim it shall make the way more evident, or give courage, or gird with fresher strength, or soothe the weariness a little, or guard from danger, I shall be glad and thankful.

Wayland Hoyt.

CONTENTS.

	PAGE.
PREPARATORY YEARS.	7
WHEN GOD HELPS	18
TEST OF LOVE.	26
PERSONAL INFLUENCE	32
MISINTERPRETATION	42
DOING GOOD	48
CONTACT WITH JESUS.	57
WHERE THE CHURCH STANDS	63
A LESSON FROM THE LILIES.	68
HOLDING POWER	71
CHARACTER AND TRIAL	76
THE BEST LAST	84
FAITH	88
PRAYER.	96
PRAYER AND FAITH	104
FAITH AND RESULTS.	110
DOUBT.	115
RESOURCES	124
WAITING ON THE LORD	130
IDOLIZING.	135

	PAGE.
CONCERNING SIN	141
DIVINE REMEDY FOR SIN	146
CHRIST THE LIGHT	151
TRUE SELF-INTEREST	156
CONQUERING THE PROMISE	161
PRAYER DENIED YET ANSWERED	168
RESOURCE IN TROUBLE	180
ALL THINGS WORKING TOGETHER FOR GOOD	185
THE MEN NEEDED	192
HOW TO BE A CHRISTIAN	197
DIVINE LOVE	200
MORAL DISINCLINATION	209
INCREASE	218
"THE SUNDAYS OF MAN'S LIFE"	230
SUCCESS	233
THE INNER SPRING	237
GOD'S METHOD	244
GRIEVING THE SPIRIT	247
THE FADING LEAF	252
CHRIST AND THE GRAVE	260

ALONG THE PILGRIMAGE.

PREPARATORY YEARS.

THE question is, What practical suggestions for ourselves may we find in the preparatory years of Jesus? These suggestions surely among others.

There is in these preparatory years a suggestion of *the intimate and vital sympathy of the Lord Jesus with all tired men and women, with all longing and waiting men and women.*

Certainly that is a most blessed Scripture: "For we have not an High Priest which cannot be touched with the feeling of our infirmities; but was in all points tempted like as we are, yet without sin." And what luminous commentary on this great Scripture is afforded by these preparatory years!

For, under what strain of toil are people held in this world of ours! "If I ever reach heaven, I think I shall do nothing for the first thousand years but rest," said a tired woman. Bending over sewing-machines; tasked with children; bowing beneath burdens of business; delving; building; searching in studious thought; anxious, too, about the results and proceeds of their toil; wondering whether they can make the ends of years buckle together; thinking how they can feed the hungry demands clamoring on every side,—what multitudes of men and women are strained and tired thus!

And in just this sometimes tasking tyranny of toil, their Lord stands with them as he went toiling on through the preparatory years. Though he was not a father, he knew parental cares and burdens. The strong probability is that Joseph died long before Jesus touched the verge of a young manhood; and so on him came the responsibilities of the family provision. And Holman Hunt is right, when in that great picture, "The Shadow of the Cross," he makes our Lord assume an attitude of one utterly wearied with a long day's toil.

And then how *waiting* is the common case of multitudes in this world of ours! How frequently the promise of some rich result now to be caught, held, delighted in, spoken to our ear, is broken to our hope! How often deferred hope makes sick hearts! How often there is a feeling in us of something loftier, nobler, we ought to do, we long to do, we mean to do, even as such feeling stirred in the heart of the boy Jesus in the Temple! And then, how the feeling seems caged and crowded down and baffled by the narrow place in which it is given us to stand; and we must wait!

There is a very noble sermon by a great preacher on the "Withheld Completions of Life." How the title of the sermon tells life's common story! How like is life to a garden of buds which tardily come to bloom, if, indeed, they come to bloom at all! And we—how long and real, and often even tragically sad, the ache of the *waiting* for the blooming!

Bunyan waiting for the opening of the gates of Bedford jail; Judson waiting for the first convert, as he toiled there at the leveling of the black, awful mountain of Eastern Heathenism; Morse waiting for a little help that he might string his telegraph wires from Washington to Baltimore, and show men how he had found a road along which the lightning would travel with docility, and lend its swiftness to the transmission of men's thoughts—ah, how much of life is consumed in waiting, and how hard the waiting is and strange!

And now our Lord comes to stand himself with us in our waiting. Lo! eighteen years went widening on between that youthful prophetic feeling in the Temple and the fulfillment and actualization of the feeling in the public and active duties of Messiahship. And, compared with the whole brief space of the active life of Jesus, how long that waiting!

Ah, what help here for tired people and for waiting people! The Christ, a Christ of toil; the Christ, a Christ of waiting. How easy and how reasonable to cry into the heart of such close sympathy:

> Be near us when we climb or fall;
> Ye watch, like God, the rolling hours,
> With larger, other eyes than ours,
> To make allowance for us all.

There is in these preparatory years of Jesus a suggestion of *the high dignity of what we call lowly service.*

Just a poor cube of stone and plaster, lighted by the door, possibly by a single window, with a room serving at once for work-room, for kitchen, for bedroom, having for furniture a mat, some cushions on the ground, one or two earthen vessels, and perhaps a painted chest. I am sure the poorest of us would call it a very poor and meager way of living. Vast difference between such home and the golden streets of heaven and the throne of the Highest, before which the shining hosts fall in worship, and toward which they send rolling on the vast volume of their praises. And in that room the Lord of heaven, with his hands roughened with humble toil, his brow beaded with the sweat of lowly industry, his back burdened with the weight of common and earthly care! Only a Galilean carpenter, only a carpenter of Nazareth, the meanest town of Galilee, the Only Begotten of the Divine Father; and yet there, at that lowly work and in that lowly life, engaged about the Father's business!

How often does it happen that we grow dissatisfied with our daily work, and fretful at that which is given us to do! That which makes up the common and routine life seems frequently so insignificant; buying, selling, learning, teaching, preaching, tending children, caring about the ten thousand infinitesimals that gather around the family. We long for a higher sphere. We pant for loftier and larger place. We say to ourselves: "My life is being wasted where I am; it is becoming worn into useless shreds; it is going for nothing."

We want to do some large business for the great Father; and, before we know it, thinking thus with ourselves, we are bitter with discontent and unnerved with despondency; and jealousy toward those who seem to be doing nobler work than we poisons and sours all the springs of life.

But Christ was doing the Father's business there at Nazareth, following his trade of carpenter and providing for the necessities of Mary's household, just as really as when, afterward, he preached the Sermon on the Mount, or raised Lazarus from the dead.

There is such a thing as lofty dignity in what we call lowly service. Oh! to learn this lesson and put it into practice. Oh! to enter into the divine philosophy of life, and understand how it is never so much what we do, *as the spirit in which we do it*, which constitutes it really divine service, the Father's business. Oh! to be able to make work worship, and to know how to write above the driest, dustiest task, "For thy sake, O Father!"

> A servant with this clause,
>   Makes drudgery divine;
> Who sweeps a room as for God's laws
>   Makes that and th' action fine.

There is in these preparatory years of Jesus a

suggestion as to *the way of entrance into a Nobler Future.*

Pity the man or woman before whose vision there does not pass and flash an ideal, putting to shame the actual, and stirring longings irrepressible toward its actualization. Such are to grow as trees do; they are not to be content to hug the earth, but they are all the time to stand with firmer trunk, flinging out more multitudinous branches to the breeze, and reaching up further toward the sun.

The what-is, however fair and bright, ought never to be but as the dim prophecy of the what-is-to-be.

The Galilean carpenter may not remain only a Galilean carpenter. He misses the doing the Father's business, if he remain such.

But this is the question: How may we enter a better future? How shall the present be made but a prophecy, which shall fulfill itself in a nobler to-come? Let me speak it reverently. How shall the boy of twelve, doing the Father's business there in Nazareth, rise into the business appropriate for the man of thirty, and accomplish it as Teacher of the people, in Gethsemane, on the cross?

Here is a clerk on a narrow salary, driven with work, pinched in pocket, and at the beck of others. Visions of a future pass before him, of a brighter time, of a commanding influence, of the largeness of a competence. Right. It is the safety of the boot-black on the street, that he hopes one day to be a millionaire. Find the boy before whom no such hope flashes, and you may at once put him among your dangerous classes. But how shall the poor clerk rise? Through driveling and carelessness, through the refusal to honestly earn his little pay because now he can get no better? That is the road downward, not upward.

We can only do larger work for the Father in the future as we are faithful in doing smaller work for him in the present. It was Jesus, faithful to the Father's business in the carpenter's shop, who was faithful to the Father's business on the cross. It is the faithful doing of what is small that shall lead us into the capacity and possibility of doing what is great. For an act is not something simply done. When a tree folds forth a leaf, it is not simply that another leaf is waving in the air. From the deepest rootlet up to the topmost branch on which that leaf is swinging, the tree is stronger.

Acts are the folding forth of character; and as the act is bad or good, well done or ill, is the character stronger and fitter for higher ends, or deteriorated and nearer destruction.

The boy doing the Father's business at twelve did the Father's loftier business at thirty, *because* he did the Father's lowlier business at twelve.

> I count this thing to be grandly true;
>   That a noble deed is a step toward God,
>   Lifting the soul from the common sod
> To a purer air and a broader view.
>
> We rise by things that are under our feet,
>   By what we have mastered of good and gain,
>   By the pride deposed and the passion slain,
> And the vanquished ills that we hourly meet.
>
> Heaven is not reached at a single bound;
>   But we build the ladder by which we rise
>   From the lowly earth to the vaulted skies;
> And we mount to its summit round by round.

And lest your life should seem to you nothing *but* a preparation in the faithful doing of lowly and little things; lest you should think you can never rise to any nobler future of lordlier service; lest you should say there can never be for me in life any higher destiny than that, with horny hand, I grasp the tools of what men call a common handicraft,—then remember that this life of ours is but the poor and meager vestibule of life's real transcendent temple, and that faithfulness here is preparation for glorious ability and infinite reward there. "Behold I come quickly, to give unto every man according as his *work* shall be." We are justified by faith; but in that heaven which we reach along the path of faith we are rewarded according to our works.

WHEN GOD HELPS.

THINK a little of the passage of the Israelites across the raging torrent of the Jordan. It is full of suggestion concerning when and how divine help may be expected.

The Israelites were to *go forth*. They were not to wait to think about it. They were not to promise they would try, and go down to the Jordan, and look at it, and perhaps wade in a little way to feel how deep and swift the waters were, and then to hurry back to camp and dry themselves, and say they had tried and could not. They were not to enter into scientific calculation of the width and deepness of the river before they should go forth. They were not first to determine to understand just how God was going to help them over—the method and the mechanism of this assistance. They were absolutely and unreservedly to commit themselves to this crossing over. They were to break up their camp on the eastern side of Jordan. They were to move onward. They were to veritably march toward that raging flood.

Also, they were to go forth *according to direction*. They were not to rush on in a hap-hazard, irregular, pellmell way. They were to go forth marshaled. Before them the priests and Levites were to bear the sacred ark. Between the ark and the ordered hosts was to be kept a space of two thousand cubits—about three-quarters of a mile—so that the ark could be held in the full view of all of them, none crowding in to shut off from any this symbol and certainty of God's presence with them. When the Israelites saw the ark of the covenant of the Lord their God, and the priests, the Levites, bearing it, then they were to remove from their places and go after it in this regulated, commanded way, and in no other.

Also, they were to go forth *in faith in the promise*. This was to be the reason of their going forth—this and nothing other, their faith in the promise. They had a promise for their going forth. "And it shall come to pass," said Joshua, "as soon as the soles of the feet of the priests that bear the ark of the Lord, the Lord of all the earth, shall rest in the waters of the Jordan, that the waters of the Jordan shall be cut off from the waters that come down from above, and they shall stand upon a heap."

The Israelites were to go forth believing that promise; so believing it that they were willing and ready to risk themselves upon it. They were to fight their skepticism with the promise. They were to smite down their anxious questionings with the weapon of the promise. They were to lay low their scientific and theological wonderings as to how it could be, as to how it could come to pass, by the cleaving sword-edge of the promise. They had nothing else. They were to expect nothing else. They had no experience of any previous crossing that Jordan in such a way. "For ye have not passed this way heretofore," said Joshua. But they did have the promise, and they were to lay grip by faith upon that.

And so these Israelites did go forth. Beyond, raged and rioted the Jordan. They marched on. Still swept on the river, freshet-filled to its utmost brim. They marched on. There is no lessening of the volume of the waters; still do the waves plunge on triumphantly; nothing could live amidst them; there is not the slightest sign that they are held in curb by the divine hand. Still they march on. I wonder if they did not question with each other. I think they must have done it, because they were men and women like ourselves. Perhaps they said to each other, "There is no sign; those raging waves are just as terrible; they would sweep away and drown us all—our wives and our little children—if we were once caught in their wild wrap; I wonder, if the waters are going to subside, why they do not begin it; but they do not; this is getting terrible; this is a great strain for faith." I think it not unlikely that they talked thus to each other because it *was* a strain for faith. They were men and women like ourselves.

And yet they have still faith enough in the promise to keep moving on toward the Jordan, and they do still march on.

But now the priests bearing Jehovah's ark have reached the margin. See, still, they go on unfalteringly. See again, the wild waters lave their feet as they touch the river's brink. And now, as that water touches *their feet* only, how strange and wonderful the sight! God's hand has surely caught those raging floods. They stop. They pile themselves on one side in a massive, watery wall, and the water still in the channel of the river hastens onward, to lose itself in the salt waves of the Dead Sea. The channel is disclosed. It is bare, utterly. It is a safe crossing. Now the priests bearing Jehovah's ark move onward to take their stand in the middle of the channel. For the whole host the crossing is easy now. On either side the ark, they stream onwards and they stream over. In a few hours they have safely crossed. They are all in Canaan.

When, then, does God help us? When we,

actually going forth in duty as he has told us, according to the directions he has given, laying hold by faith upon his promise, come to the limit of our strength—when thus our feet are dipped in the brim of the waters of our Jordan, his great help does come.

It comes in difficult duty. Duty—that is something due; due—that is something owed; owed —that is something one ought. You are conscious of this feeling of oughtness. But it is something difficult, like that Jordan. Notwithstanding, go forth, as God has ordered, in the faith of his promise, and help shall fall.

It comes *scattering foreboded sorrow.* Do you not remember how the women, going to the sepulchre asked anxiously, "Who shall roll away the stone?" but going on, even though the great stone crossed their pathway, found it rolled away?

It comes *in death.* Mr. Greatheart was telling Mr. Honest of Mr. Fearing, whom, after the king's direction, he had guided to the celestial city. Said Mr. Greatheart, "Mr. Fearing was one that played upon the bass; I have heard that he lay roaring at the Slough of Despond for above a month together; nor durst he, for all he saw several go over before him, venture, though they, many of them, offered to lend him their hands. He would not go back neither. 'The celestial city,' he said,—'he should die if he came not to it.' And yet he was dejected at every difficulty, and stumbling at every straw that any one cast in his way. Well, after he had lain at the Slough of Despond awhile, as I told you, one sunshiny morning, I do not know how, he ventured, and so got over; but when he was over, he would scarcely believe it. But when he was come to the river where there was no bridge, there again he was in a heavy case. Now, now, he said, he should be drowned forever, and so never see that face in comfort that he had come so many miles to behold. And here also," continued Mr. Greatheart, "I took notice of what was very remarkable,—the water of that river *was lower at this time than I ever saw it in all my life,* so he went over at last not much above wet-shod."

Also look at this truth of the divine help in the direction of *conversion*. There is that Jordan of belief in Jesus, of the absolute commitment of the self to him which we must pass before we can enter the Canaan of forgiveness, and God's favor, and the noble life. Now go on toward it. Cross it. But you have no feeling, you say; that is not to the matter. But you do not know such feeling as other people say they have; that is not to the matter. But you do not understand how it can be; you need not; that is not to the matter. But you are not fit to make the crossing; you never will be fitter; that is not to the matter. This is enough. God tells you to go forth. "Except a man be born again, he cannot see the kingdom of God." God tells you the way: "Him that cometh unto me." God gives you his promise: "I will not cast out." Go forth, then, along his way in faith of his promise; and when your feet but touch the brim of a perfect self-surrender, you are his, you are Christian. His forgiveness falls, you have passed into the Canaan of the new life.

TEST OF LOVE.

EVERMORE the Test of Love is *Service*. "Simon Peter, lovest thou me?" asked Jesus. "Lord, thou knowest all things; thou knowest that I love thee." "Serve me then," said Jesus; "feed my lambs; shepherd my sheep; feed my little sheep."

Service is the test which discriminates the empty and idle sentimentality of love from the actuality and noble stringency of it.

This is the commonest of truths, and yet it is a truth of which in religion we need constantly to be reminded. There in that great poem of Spenser's "Faerie Queen," when the brave knight who attended the gentle lady and protected her and fought for her, was sadly wounded in the conflict in her behalf, and then when she gave herself to utmost care for him, and stained her fair white fingers with the blood issuing from his wounds, and, to those remonstrating with her that she should thus stain and redden her beautiful fairness, it is a touch true to nature when Spenser makes her reply, "Entire affection hateth nicer hands."

Of course that is a touch true to nature. You recognize it such at once. That is not love; it is only the sickly sham and sentimentality and semblance of it, which will refuse to do hard things for the object of its affection. An *entire* affection always "hateth nicer hands." Its thought is not of self, except as self can use itself in any sort of service for the object of love.

Well, that which is true of a real love everywhere, is just as true of a real religious love. That is not a religious love whose hands are too nice to be lent to strenuous, difficult, even painful service.

She was a heathen convert. She was a solitary lamp burning in that darkness. She had her Testament, and that was all—no church, no school, no Christian friend. But when the great missionary, Moffat, came to that village on the banks of the Orange River, in South Africa, and when the heathen people of the village roughly bade him and his companions, hungry and thirsty and tired, halt at a distance, and would sell them neither food nor water, and when this poor black convert brought them milk, and water, and flesh, and wood for fire, sobbing out, as the tears rolled down her dark cheeks, "I love him whose you are, and surely it is my duty to give you a cup of cold water in his name; my heart is full, therefore I cannot speak the joy I feel in this out-of-the-world place;" why, then this poor black convert gave the real test of the love she bore her Lord in *service* to those who loved him also, in service for him rendered to them. Of course, you say, that is true; I believe in her; she was a true convert, because she had true love, and she manifested the test for love in service.

And the test for love is even *difficult* service. Certainly that is not a masterful love which is hindered in its service by difficulty. Certainly it would not always be easy for Peter to shepherd

Christ's sheep. Sometimes, the sheep would be wandering and unruly, and straying into forbidden places, to be gone after in self-denying journeying, and to be won back by pains and prayers. Certainly it would not always be easy for Peter to find Christ's little sheep. Sometimes youth is boisterous, and impatient of control, and defiant of authority; and Peter must draw the rein on his own natural impetuosity and quick temper, and be self-controlled, and loving, and strongly gentle. It was not very easy service which Christ made the test of Peter's love. But love which will not take hold of even jagged duty, is no love, in the sense Christ meant, when he said, "Simon, son of Jonas, lovest thou me?"

He professes to love, but he gave up his Sunday-school class because he could not see that he was doing much good in it. He was not willing to sow patiently for the sake of Christ, and trust him for the reaping. I wonder if action and reason like that were evidence of a true love.

He professes to love, but he gave up his class because his scholars worried him, it was hard work to interest them, and he did not like the hard work for Christ's sake. I wonder if action and reason like that were evidence of a true love.

He professes to love, but he gave up his class because the superintendent unintentionally hurt his feelings; he did not think it pleasant; and he did not like to endure unpleasantness for Christ's sake. I wonder if action and reason like that were evidence of a true love!

He professes to love, but he gave up his class because he did not get just the place he wanted in the school, and so thought himself passed by and underrated. He could not work in a lowly place for Christ. I wonder if action and reason like that were evidence of a true love.

He professes to love, and really he can teach, he has peculiar gifts for teaching, he has time, his Lord has variously blessed him much, but he will not teach. He likes too well a vacant Sunday afternoon; or he has graduated from such work now in his later years; or he wants to indulge himself in something which would not set a good example for his scholars, should he teach; or he has an undefined disinclination, for which he cannot or does not want to assign definite reason. Oh, I wonder if action and reason like these are evidence of a true love!

And all the time the test of love is service, can be nothing else. "Do you love the Saviour, son of Jonas?" says Jesus; "then *do* something for me; feed my lambs, shepherd my sheep, feed my little sheep."

Ah, it is solemn truth. If to our protestation of love we do not respond in some real service, then our love is pinchbeck, it is counterfeit, it is mimicry, it is simulation, it is travesty, it is seeming, it is sham—it is not Love.

PERSONAL INFLUENCE.

THERE is a kind of hidden truth in what the Scripture tells us of the relation of John the Baptist with his disciples, which a little explanation will bring out, and which, when brought out, is most suggestive.

John the Baptist, you will remember, was a great and controlling preacher. His intense, awakening words stirred all Judea into attention. To the Jordan bank, which was his pulpit; to the wilderness, which was his sanctuary—the people crowded. Everywhere, in every one's heart, there was longing and waiting for some great new deliverer. The people believed that they were standing at the ending point of prophecy; that in some other and new way God would break his silence and speak to them by the tongue of his Messiah.

The stir in the wilderness caused answering

stir among religious leaders at Jerusalem. Perhaps this original and heart-awakening prophet might be himself Messiah. The Sanhedrim choose a deputation to visit John, that they may question him and satisfy themselves. "This is the record of John, when the Jews sent priests and Levites to Jerusalem to ask him, Who art thou? And he confessed and denied not, but confessed, I am not the Christ. And they asked What then, art thou Elias? And he saith, I am not." He really was the prophet who in the twilight before Messiah's rising was *to stand for* the old, grim, strong Elijah. The prophet Malachi had declared that Elijah was to come just before Messiah. The Lord Jesus afterward distinctly said that John the Baptist was the Elijah foretold by Malachi, and rightfully expected by the people. I suppose the true explanation is, as some one else has suggested, that, like any other great but humble messenger of God, John the Baptist did not comprehend his own character and mission in relation to ancient prophecy. He was more than he thought he was. It is vastly better to be more than you think you are, than to think yourself more than you are. God's best servants are always those who are careless about great names and places for themselves—who think first and chiefest of doing God's work and will in the places in which he has given them to stand. In one of Robert Browning's poems, the angel Gabriel is imagined taking the place of a poor earth-born boy, because it was God's will that he should do it; and in this way the poet sings about the angel:

> Then to his poor trade he turned,
> By which his daily bread was earned;
> And ever o'er the trade he bent,
> And ever on the earth content.
> *He did God's will.* To him all one
> If on the earth or in the sun.

For you see, when you come to the true thought about it, the place of God's will is heaven, whether it is down here or up yonder.

Then this committee from the Sanhedrim went on to ask John the Baptist, "Art thou that prophet?" And he answered, "No." The Jews expected a prophet, other than Elijah, who should precede the Messiah; which expectation was based on a certain prediction in Deuteronomy. They made a mistake in their interprettation. Where Moses speaks of a prophet whom God should raise up from the midst of them like unto Moses, and unto whom they should hearken, they thought Moses was referring to some prophet other than the blessed Messiah himself, to whom the prophecy did refer really. When the prophecy *has been matched* by its fulfillment, it is easy then to see the matching; and as a proof that "holy men of old spake as they were moved by the Holy Ghost," your fulfilled prophecy becomes a proof immensely strong. But it is a difficult and dangerous thing to look into an *unfulfilled* prophecy and say it means precisely this and this, and it is going to come to its fulfillment precisely so, and precisely then. Let us beware of doing that concerning the commotions in our world, concerning the second coming of our Lord. We are to believe in the second coming of our Lord—that, unfulfilled prophecy distinctly asserts; but precisely how, and precisely when, it is not given us to know; and concerning it, it is very dangerous for us to make assertion.

Well, this committee reply to John: "Who art thou, that we may give an answer to them that sent us? What sayest thou of thyself?" And then John answers: "About all that I know about myself is that I am somehow the fulfillment of Isaiah's prophecy of a voice that should come crying in the wilderness, 'Make straight the way of the Lord.' I am sure the Messiah is coming; I am sure there are multitudes of things that ought to be straightened for his coming. This is who I am, and all I am. I am the voice crying in the wilderness, 'Make straight the way of the Lord.'" John's answer was not very satisfactory to these people from Jerusalem. Perhaps the voice forced itself rather uncomfortably into the crooked places in their lives, and made them think that they would have a good deal of straightening to do themselves before the coming of the Messiah could be a very welcome thing to them. I wonder if none of us feel in that way about our Lord's coming to us by death, or by his flaming second advent. I wonder if we have not a pretty large duty of straightening to do. This committee asked John various questions about his baptism; but he does not have much to say to them except concerning the great and certain coming One, of whose advent he is only herald. So the deputation return to Jerusalem.

Then the verses of the Scripture here seem to go on to tell us of a *public discourse* of John, preached to the people crowding around, the next day after the visit of this deputation from the Sanhedrim. Jesus himself comes toward him amid the throng, and as John sees him, he exclaims, "Behold the Lamb of God, which taketh away the sins of the world." John identifies this Jesus as the one who, coming after him, is preferred before him. All this *public* sermon of John's here to the crowd, is a sermon of distinct speech, and of tender, earnest pointing toward the Lamb of God who beareth away the sins of the world, and who was standing veritably there among the people. Nothing could be stronger, nothing could be plainer, nothing could be more convincing, than this public speech of John's about the Lamb of God.

But the thing I would like to have you notice about this public sermon of John's is that, as far as the record goes—and like many a clear and yearning sermon that has been preached since the time of that public service in the wilderness—the sermon seems to have made no appreciable impression whatsoever. We do not read that the sermon resulted in the accepting and following of the Lamb of God then by anybody. The throng heard it; as far as we know, they simply heard it—they did not act on it. John's special disciples heard it; as far as we know, they simply heard it—they did not act on it. The public service appeared to come to nothing. The people listened, and as far as we can find out, that is all they did.

We have come up now to the special truth on which I would fix your attention. Will you be kind enough particularly to notice these words:

"Again the next day after"—that is, the next day after this public sermon about the Lamb of God who beareth away the sins of the world—John stood and two of his disciples. The throng were all gone now. There was no public preaching going on. John was just then in solitude, and there were with him only two of his disciples. And looking upon Jesus as he walked—as we would say, as he was taking a walk—as another suggests, one of the numerous indications in the gospel that Christ was a lover of nature and accustomed to meditate and study in communion with nature—in the ordering of Divine Providence just then, when John stands alone with two of his disciples, Jesus comes walking by. And now John immediately follows up the thought of the public sermon he had preached the day before, by *private* and *personal* speech and influence. And looking upon Jesus as he walked, he said, "Behold the Lamb of God." And what the public sermon did not seem to do, the private and personal word, following up the public teaching of the sermon, did do; for we read immediately that the two disciples heard him speak, *and they followed Jesus.* What public effort did not seem to accomplish, private effort did.

And it is a remarkable fact that this first chapter of John's Gospel which, in the latter part of it, tells us of the first conquering of men to Christ, discloses as the weapon of that conquering, not the great and public gathering and religious service, but through the whole course of it the victorious arm of a personal and private influence. Just see; these first disciples are led into following Christ, not by a public, general speech, but by the private, personal words of John the Baptist. "One of the two which heard John speak and followed him was Andrew, Simon Peter's brother. He first findeth his own brother Simon." Simon Peter is brought to Christ by the private and personal influence of his brother Andrew. "The day following, Jesus would go forth into Galilee, and findeth Philip and saith unto him, Follow me." It is the private and personal influence of Christ which calls and clasps Philip to himself. "Philip findeth Nathanael."

And so the private and personal influence of Philip captures Nathanael. Archimedes, when he made one of his discoveries, rushed out into the street exclaiming, "Eureka! Eureka! I have found it! I have found it!" Archbishop Trench calls this a chapter of Eurekas. Andrew findeth Messiah, then Andrew findeth Simon his brother, then Jesus findeth Philip, then Philip findeth Nathanael." It is a chapter of findings, and it is all through the findings of a private and personal influence. This then is the truth we come to: the value and the victory of personal work and personal influence.

Ministers ought to remember this. When the public sermon seems to fail, let them follow it up by personal, pastoral work.

Sunday-school teachers should remember this. What seems to be failure before others and in the class-room, may be changed into shining success by the tender, personal private word.

MISINTERPRETATION.

WE are told in John's Gospel that our Lord Christ needed not that any should testify of man, for he knew what was in man. There is vast comfort in this fact, in view of the frequent misinterpretations of life. I think that is a most significant sentence, which I met some time since from Meta Klopstock: "It may be that an action displeases us which would please us if we knew its true aim and whole extent." But precisely what may be this true aim and whole extent of an action which somebody may do, we do not know; and what is worse, blinded perhaps by prejudice; or bitter and censorious with grudge; or allowing ourselves in the vile habit of a constant and captious criticism, we do not seek to know. We only, out of hand, declare the motive mean and the aim bad.

Considering the constant and tremendous

denunciation of the Scripture against the evil judgment of others, against slandering, against a slashing, slaughtering gossip about others, it is even frightful to think how blatantly and with what slight qualms of conscience even professedly Christian people offend in this manner, which men are apt to think so slight, but which the Scripture calls so great.

There was a poor Arab once who, traveling in the desert, and accustomed only to water from muddied and brackish wells, came upon a spring of the purest and sweetest water. So fresh and pure did the water seem to him that he thought it a not unworthy present to the Caliph of his tribe. And so, filling his water-skin to the full with it, he started on a long and difficult journey to his Caliph's presence. At last he laid his gift of the sweet water at his monarch's feet. The Caliph did not despise the poor man's offering; ordered some of it poured into a cup; drank it; presented the humble giver with a suitable reward. The courtiers, crowding around, were making haste themselves to taste the wonderful water, but the Caliph immediately forbade them—not a drop of it might they touch. When, at last, the humble man had gone, the courtiers ventured to ask the reason of a command so strange. Then the Caliph answered:

"During the travels of the Arab, the water in his leathern bottle had become impure and distasteful; but it was an offering of love, and as such I received it with pleasure; but I well knew that had I allowed another to partake of it, he would not have concealed his disgust; and therefore I forbade you to touch the water, lest the heart of the poor man should have been wounded."

What righteous and subtly kind appreciation of the real extent and true aim of the poor man's action! How different this from the too usual action! The too usual action would have been for the Caliph, on tasting it, to have made a face of disgust himself, and then to have handed the cup of the spoiled water to everybody about, for them to taste and make faces too. The pure and precious motive of the act would have been overslaughed, unappreciated, counted for nothing.

A brother had been grieved, and the rest would have had the mean satisfaction of making faces.

Right here emerges, and so needlessly, a vast amount of the pain of life. It is right here that so many of us make needless and bitter pain for others. Behind the act we will not be at the trouble to go, to see if we cannot find a transfiguring motive. No, too often we ruthlessly and heedlessly, in our thought, change a good act into a bad, because we constantly allow ourselves in the miserable and malicious habit of almost always supposing in some people a bad motive.

Once on a Christmas time, there was sent the poet Whittier a gentian pressed between two panes of glass. Looked at from one side, you saw but a poor blurred mass of something. But looked at from the other side, you saw the exquisite flower, delicately outlined. Suppose the poet had persisted in looking at it only from the blurred side. That is the way some people will persistently look at the well-meant actions of their fellows. But the poet would not. And this is the way he sings about it:

The time of gifts has come again,
And on my northern window pane,
Outlined against the day's brief flight,
A Christmas token hangs in sight.
The wayside travelers, as they pass,
Mark the gray disc of clouded glass;
And the dull blankness seems, perchance,
Folly to their wise ignorance.

They cannot from their outlook see
The perfect grace it has for me;
For there, the flower whose fringes through
The frosty breath of autumn blew,
Turns from without its face of bloom
To the warm tropic of my room,
As fair as when beside its brook
The hue of bending skies it took.

But deeper meanings come to me,
My half-immortal flower, from thee;
Man judges from a partial view,
None ever yet his brother knew.
The Eternal Eye that sees the whole
May better read the darkened soul,
And find, to outward sense denied,
The flower upon its inmost side.

And oftener than we think it, there is a flower upon the inmost side of action. And the trouble with many of us is, that we will neither suppose it there, nor take the least pains in looking for it.

And so we constantly misinterpret those who touch us, and become to all around, fountains, not of pleasant, but of bitter waters.

But now, for any pierced with this pain of misinterpretation, there is the comfort of a resource and a refuge. There is One who knows us with a knowledge penetrating, with a knowledge perfect. The Lord Christ needs not that any should testify of man, for he knows what is in man. The Lord Christ never misinterprets.

>Oh, comfort one another;
>For the way is growing dreary,
>The feet are often weary,
>And the heart is very sad—
>There is heavy burden-bearing,
>When it seems that none are caring,
>And we half forget that ever we were glad.

DOING GOOD.

THE method of Christ with that woman at the well's mouth in Samaria, is full of suggestion about this matter.

Christ *used personal contact.* Here was the woman coming to draw water; here was Christ sitting weary and thirsty on the well. "Give me to drink," said the Master. At once Christ established a personal relation between that woman and himself. It became face to face and heart to heart work immediately. A warm heart, stirred with solicitude for another, and set close up against that other heart—this is the mightiest force for good in the wide world. If you will look thoughtfully back along your lives, you will find that you have been moulded oftener and more completely by the close contact of separate persons with yourself than by any other influence whatsoever. Character magnetizes character. Hearts fashion to their own shape others against which they have set themselves.

Now, this power of personal contact, so controlling everywhere else, is as mighty in religion. Yet I am sure it is just this energy of personal contact which the church misses most the use of. I know, and I am thankful, that the church of to-day is strenuously active in many ways and many directions. I know that girdling the globe there is a zodiac of mission stations. I know that there are well conducted and well adjusted and nobly manned societies and boards, with regal revenues for the furtherance of Christianity. I know that all these are needful and must be carried on, and illimitably enlarged both in sphere and resource. But is it not true that the religion of to-day is one which does not closely enough follow the Saviour in his example of personal contact? Is it not true that the religion of to-day in its forth-putting energies is one too much by proxy? Is it not true that we are too ready to trust to incorporated and imposing machineries; too ready to delegate to some Board or to some minister what should be given into the consecrated hands of the royal priesthood of the whole church?

A church wants a minister. Forthwith the country is scoured for a man who will draw. Then when he is gotten and does it, possibly by means of a bad sensationalism, men cry success, and the thing is left to run. But is it not as much the duty of the church to fill its building and bring outside people under the influence of religion as it is the minister's? The minister is but one; the church is many. The minister and the church are to be workers together for Christ. Between every member of the church and every one who has not yielded his heart to Jesus there should be established this relation of personal contact. The Christ within the heart is to be an outreaching Christ. Your Christian life is faulty if it be not pressed with yearning to make some other person Christian.

The Sunday-school is a noble institution. I hail every possible influence which can increase its vitality and efficiency; yet I sometimes fear there is many a parent who so uses the Sunday-school that he transmutes it from a blessing to an evil. He sends his child to the Sunday-school, and that is all he does. He divests himself of religious responsibility toward his child. He commits the vast matter of the Christian culture of his own child to some Sunday-school teacher, whom likely enough he does not even know. He says when he thinks about it, "Oh, the Sunday-school teacher will take care of that." He enters into no personal religious contact with his children. He speaks to them religiously never. He prays with them personally and pleadingly never.

But not thus by any careless way of proxy can the church conquer the world, and bring in the glad millennial time. Christ sets before us the example of personal contact. Upon every member of the church, from the littlest to the loftiest, this duty devolves. Christianity is democratic. Neither are its privileges nor its duties delegated to any special, sceptered, sacred, priestly class. Ye are all a royal priesthood.

For every member there is priestly service. No Christian man is doing Christian duty until he forms this relation of personal contact with some unchristian heart, to point it to Jesus Christ, by whom the lost is saved.

Also, in thus pointing this poor woman to himself and so saving her, Christ *used passing opportunities*. A momentary resting place in the weary journey, the well's mouth, the woman coming to draw water, the thirst of the traveler, —very slight matters in themselves, and yet these slight matters were moulded into the occasion for that marvelous conversation in which the sinful, thirsting heart of that poor woman caught sight of the gleam of the eternal waters. The Lord Jesus did not idly wait for some precious opportunity. He compelled passing events into precious opportunity. To do this—to become alert and skillful in seizing the passing chance— is a very high religious attainment. It can be done only as religion is a most vital and overcoming force in one's own heart. But if it be thus with a man, it is an easy matter. "No work is drudgery except to the unwilling worker."

In other years, in the White Mountains, I used to meet a queer old man, who believed he knew all about the true formation of the earth, inside and outside. The earth, he declared, is a hollow globe, inhabited within as well as without. Wherever there is water outside there is land inside, and wherever there is water inside there is land outside, and so on. Of course, it was a very foolish theory; but I was often much interested and amused in noticing how utterly full the old man was of it, and how naturally he made everything you might converse with him about, only another path to the discussion of his favorite subject. Every grass-blade led to it, every rock, every running brook, the clouds in the sky. Neither did there seem to be anything forced or unnatural about it. The old gentleman was so surcharged with his thought that it was like water confined, seeking egress everywhere. It was thus with the old man, because there was so much of it in the old man.

If we were only so full of the power and peace of our religion, every passing event would be a passing chance of preaching. Along the path of every one there would spring up multitudes of opportunities. There would be set up multitudes of pulpits. It was thus always with the Lord Christ. To him the lily taught trust. The city on the hill was emblematic of Christian influence. The leaven in the dough meant regenerative force. The branches of the vine taught the Christian dependence on his Lord. The water which the woman came to draw was shining with hints of that water of which if a man drink, he shall never thirst. Thus each slightest thing, each smallest event, was transfigured by the Lord into opportunity for the telling forth of truth.

Also, in the pointing this woman to himself that he might save her, Christ *used personal friendliness*. She was a Samaritan, and was therefore filled with all possible and bitter prejudice against a Jew. She was a tarnished woman, standing despoiled of a precious purity, yet Christ showed himself at once her friend. Others might fling her off, others might curl the lofty lip, but Christ did not. "Give me to drink," he said. Receiving a drink from one meant more in the Oriental fashion of society than it does with us. It was the seal and the signal of friendship. When Christ asked her for that water, he meant to let her know that she could reckon him a friend. He goes further; he consents to ask a favor of her. He is willing to put himself in the position of obligation to her, if only he may save her. It will never do for you or me to stand upon some fancied height of goodness, and look down upon and lecture people. Even the sinless Jesus did not that. He was known all over as the friend of publicans and sinners, in order that the weary, wandering ones might come to him without difficulty, and easily enter the clasping of his great love.

There was in the temple of Jerusalem a gate called Beautiful. Its walls were burnished gold; its posts were glorious with richest carvings; its pavements were of rare mosaics; and along its top was flung a golden grape-vine, from whose branches hung huge clusters of precious stones. It was the masterpiece of the temple workmanship. It was the joy and pride of every worshiper within those temple walls. Every Christian church should have as well a gate Beautiful, formed, not of gold and bronze and jewels, but of something costlier. Of these should this gate Beautiful be builded—of the hearts of all the membership alive with love, putting themselves in constant contact with those who do not know their Lord; wisely alert for passing opportunity to tell of him; tender toward all with a gentle Christian friendliness, and undespairing of the worst. How through such a gate, reared thus of living and loving hearts, would multitudes of the sinful and the weary and the wayward pass, to find the pardon and peace and power which is in Jesus Christ our Lord!

CONTACT WITH JESUS.

THIS was the one absolute necessity for that man smitten with palsy, whom his friends got into Christ's presence, breaking up the roof, and letting him down before him. Doubtless, this contact with Jesus was the thing which he, in his sick misery, most desired. Certainly this was the thing which those four friends of his were determined on for him. The earnestness of those four friends to get him into this contact is very touching. They would not be baffled. The helplessness of the sick man should not baffle them; they would carry him. The thick crowd blocking the path to Jesus should not; they would try some other way. The hindering roof should not; they would break it up. Every line of the narrative vibrates, as does a harp-string when you strike it, with the intense earnestness of these men. If human strength and skill could accomplish it, this sick man, borne of four, *must be* laid at the feet of the Great Healer. I do not know a more pathetic story of intense service for another's sake in the whole Scriptures. Contact with Jesus was the imploring need; contact with Jesus, this man, smitten into more than an infant's helplessness, should anyhow and somehow have.

Now the miracles of Jesus are acted parables. They are the dramas of the gospel. They put spiritual truth into living form, and act it before your eyes. That helpless paralytic stands forth and represents an immense and race-wide spiritual fact. As helpless as the palsy was rendering him from the vigor and motion of his health physical, so helpless has sin rendered every one toward the righteous and rejoicing spiritual life which the law of God demands. Helpless toward what one should, are men and women all. Helpless toward right being and toward heaven, is, in itself, the child you love, whom you guard so tenderly, whom you would yield your life for. "Even the youths shall faint and be weary, and the young men shall utterly fail," except as they wait upon the Lord, who only can renew their strength.

And the Lord Jesus amid that crowd, speaking to that man wonderful energizing words, stands representative of another profound spiritual truth —that the sort of spiritual life which men must reach, which your children must reach, can be imparted by him only, can flow into human souls only from his pierced hands. This is what he constantly asserts for himself. This is the startling difference between him and every other religious teacher that has ever stood among men. "My doctrines are what you need," these have said. "I am what you need," he has said.

Are men helpless in spiritual darkness? Then he is the Light; the true Light; the Light come into the world; the Light of men; the Light to lighten the Gentiles. Then he is the Star; the morning Star; the bright and morning Star; the day Star; the Day-Spring from on high; the Sun of righteousness.

Are men helpless in spiritual famine? Then he is the Bread of God; the true Bread; the

Bread of heaven; the Bread which came down from heaven; the Bread of life; the living Bread; the hidden Manna.

Are men helpless and tortured in spiritual thirst? Then he is the living Water; the Well of water springing up into everlasting life, of which, if a man drink, he shall never thirst.

Are men helpless in spiritual wandering, having lost the right path and the true? Then he is the one Shepherd; the Shepherd of the sheep; the Shepherd and Bishop of souls; the good Shepherd that laid down his life for the sheep; the great Shepherd that was brought again from the dead; the chief Shepherd who shall again appear.

Are men helpless in spiritual weakness and inability? Then he is the Strength of the children of Israel; the Strength of the needy in distress; the Refuge from the storm; the Covert from the tempest; the Horn of salvation.

Are men helpless in spiritual defencelessness? Then he is the Rock; the strong Rock; the Rock of ages; the Rock higher than one's self; the Rock of our strength, of our refuge; the Habitation of my salvation; my Rock and my Redeemer.

Are men helpless before a threatened spiritual penalty of broken law? Then he is the Lamb that beareth away the sins of the world; the Lamb slain; the Priest; the High Priest; the great High Priest; the Mediator; the Propitiation for our sins; the Intercessor; the Advocate; the Surety.

Are men helpless in the fight of life for want of spiritual leadership? Then he is the Captain of salvation; the Author and Finisher of faith; the Leader and Deliverer; the Lion of the tribe of Judah; the Ensign for the people; the Chiefest among ten thousand.

Are men helpless for need of a spiritual king and governor? Then he is the King; he is King of kings; the King of righteousness; the King of peace; the King of glory; the King in his beauty, and the government is upon his shoulders.

He it is whom men need—not truths about him; Him—not creeds, which declare him; Him—not theologies, which seek to explain him; Him—not sacraments, which represent him; Him—not churches, which stand for him; Him—valuable as all these things are, they are needs secondary, not primary. The first, foremost, undermost, uppermost, underlying, over-topping need is the present Christ, dispensing his forgiveness, speaking his peace, imparting his strength, infusing his joy, promising his heaven. Personal contact with the personal Christ; this is the awful, stringent, eternity-deciding necessity for every human soul.

WHERE THE CHURCH STANDS.

"THEY had no leisure, so much as to eat." Rest was absolutely needful for the wearied Lord and his tired followers. "Come ye yourselves apart into a desert place, and rest awhile," the Master says.

They enter a boat to sail across the lake. The wind blows fresh against them. They hug the shore, and make slow advance. The multitude, left behind, see them departing, and somehow learn their destination. They see, too, how close to the land they keep and how slowly the boat is moving. They follow on foot along the shore. A few hours' brisk walking can compass the little sea. When Jesus and the disciples land, they find the restful place already peopled with those whose walking has outstripped their sailing. The crowd swells till more than five thousand men, besides the women and the children, have gathered there to Jesus with their sicknesses and sins.

There is no chance for rest. Retiring to a neighboring mountain, Jesus sits down and teaches and heals. And so the hours go on. Yet do the multitude remain. The shadows lengthen toward the night. Still Jesus teaches. Still the crowd clings. The disciples grow anxious. Perhaps they are a little petulant, that they have been robbed of the rest they need so much. Here is the multitude in this foodless and shelterless place; the night is near. What is to be done?

At length the disciples suggest to Jesus—"This is a desert place, and the time is now past; send them away, that they may go into the country round about, and into the villages, and lodge, and buy bread for themselves; for they have nothing to eat."

But the Lord answers, they need not depart; "*give ye them to eat.*"

The story need not hold us further—the consternation of the twelve, the slightness of their resource; the growth of that resource when brought to Christ, and when Christ blesses it; the more than five thousand satisfied by that which, in itself, was not enough for five.

But this mandate, "give *ye* them to eat," is singularly significant of the place to which our Lord has called his church.

Jesus does not say to the disciples, you need not trouble yourselves about this multitude; my power is broad enough and strong enough to carry them. Rather, it is precisely this he does command, that the disciples *be* troubled about the throng. Christ lays the burden of the whole vast crowd right upon the disciples. The presence of the multitude, its hunger, its shelterlessness, the thickening night,—these are just the things which the Lord moulds into a claim that the disciples may not shirk. "It is your duty to help them, and help is to come to them through you, O disciples. You are the channels of supply. You are the transmitters of the divine bounty. You stand between, and introduce to each other, the wealth of my power and the emptiness of their poverty. *Give ye them to eat.*"

Here, then, does the church stand—in this place of mediation. It is no place of mediation in the Romish sense of priest-craft and infallible authority, but it is a place of mediation in the sense of standing between divine fullness and the world's need, that they may be brought in contact.

Just as the hunger of the multitude was, in Christ's sight, a claim upon the disciples, that they should furnish food; so now, the ignorance, the darkness, the spiritual famine, the sinfulness of the world, gather themselves into a thunderous demand upon the church to give Christ to it, who only is wisdom for it, light and food, and comfort and forgiveness.

Give *ye* them to eat; you are responsible for them—the multitude of the unchurched within a stone's throw of your sanctuary; the needy at home; the needy upon distant shores.

And when our resources seem as meagerly proportioned to our duty as seemed those bits of bread and those two fishes to *those* disciples, staggering before the vast hunger of that crowd, let us remember the Christ behind the scant supply, and what he did unto it; and let us remember, too, that we can never do our duty of distribution, except, as through a joyful consecration of our resources, *we* get them greatened by his power. But the five loaves and the two fishes can become a magazine, when blessed by him.

A LESSON FROM THE LILIES.

THAT is a very beautiful fact I came upon sometime since about the lilies of the Holy Land. They grow even on the barest and stoniest spots. They last through the hardest droughts. They have large, bulbous roots, in which are packed away a reserve of nourishment, and which securely guard the principle of life. So they start up where you never expect flowers. But they do more than just grow themselves. Their broad leaves, and their large blossoms, cast a shadow and attract the moisture in the air, condensing it into dew; and so, protected by their shadow and getting fragments of their dew, other vegetations begin to flourish around and under them. Rich tufts of grass grow green about their roots, and nowhere is the herbage so luxuriant as under the shadow of these beautiful and graceful flowers.

So I think the Church of Christ ought to be like that lily in this dry and difficult world. It ought to throw protecting and healing and helping shadows. It ought to turn the stony spots into beautiful verdure, and fight away the evil barrenness. Not Young Men's Christian Associations, good as they are; not temperance societies, noble as is the work they do; not various efforts unorganized and sporadic, filled with a passing blessing as they may be; but the real agency, the divine institution, the mightiest help for the world, is the Church of the Lord Jesus.

But now the lily is an organism. It is made up of root and bulb and stem and leaf and flower. And it can only do its mediating duty, it can only rescue its patch of ground from barrenness, as all its various parts work, and work together—as root and bulb and stem and leaf and flower—each and all—work.

The church, too, is an organism. It is made up of pastor and of deacons and of membership. And this membership is very various, and variously endowed. Culture, wealth, social position, gifts of speech, gifts of persuasion, gifts of prayer, gifts of teaching, gifts of sympathy, gifts of faith, gifts of visiting—many various gifts—are variously distributed, and the church can only make its power felt, and do its duty worthily, as all its various parts work and work together; as the entire membership, pastor, deacons—all—yield themselves to service.

HOLDING POWER.

WHEN travelers are passing along the River Nile in those queer boats, with their vast sails, which have been for ages the means of navigation on that river, it makes the greatest difference whether the prow of their boat be turned from the river's mouth or toward it. If they are going toward the sources of the river, bound for Karnak or the Cataracts, they must advance against the steady current setting seaward. They must avail themselves of every favoring chance and wind; or if the winds are adverse, they must resort to the tracking of the boat, as it is called—the slow towing of it by the lazy Arab crew, walking and growling along the river banks. It is slow work—creeping along up stream.

But if they are going from the river's sources toward the sea, bound for Cairo or for Alexandria, there is no slow tracking, there is no need that much account be taken of the breezes, for all the time, steadily flowing, bearing all things on its broad bosom, sets on the strong deep current, hastening ever toward the ocean. That mighty current takes the boat in its arms and carries it on and on.

Now, any one who has ever tried to live truly, nobly, worthily, has found himself in the condition of the travelers who are beating up against the current of the Nile. Somehow, one in such a case must all the time make head against a tidal tendency. It is a sad fact about life, that it is a great deal easier to float with the underlying and ever-moving current toward the wrong, than to turn the boat of life the other way and keep it set and pushing toward the up-stream right. For right is up-stream in this world, and not down-stream. The common tendency of things is from what is highest and holiest toward the expedient, the equivocal, the evil.

I have read of voyagers up the Nile who were stuck for days in the mud, aground, who were beset by baffling winds and borne back by currents; who but crept on, inch by inch, while the Arab crew tugged, splashing, sweating, scolding, pulling at the rope, by which they just managed to draw the vessel along the shore. There is spiritual parallel here. It often seems as though we did not, and could not, make any advance.

Sometimes even the clear vision of the Christian ideal discourages us. There are times when, as the sun bursts through the mists, there flashes upon us a more shining conception of the character of Jesus. In the light of that we get a new view of our own imperfection, brokenness, weakness. A kind of paralysis falls upon our effort toward it. "What!" we say, "to become that, to be beautiful with such purity, to be lifted into such excellence, to become lovely with such sacrifice? Impossible! Such a coarse and dirty actual to rise into such an ideal? It cannot be!" And we feel the truth of that mournful verse of Schiller:

> Thither, ah, no footstep tendeth;
> There the heaven above so clear
> Never earth to touch descendeth,
> And the there is never here.

Then, too, the tug and strain toward goodness often weary. Life seems very full of trouble and very slight in peace. Besetting sins will still beset. An Irishman cut off a turtle's head. He was surprised, hours after, to see the head moving, the jaws opening and shutting. "Surely the beast is dead, but he isn't *sinsible of it*," said he. So, sometimes, the sins we thought were slain keep up their miserable lives. The old passion re-appears; the old appetite reunites its chains; the old petulance frets on; the old discontent whines on; the old distrust fears on. With David, we are weary with our groaning; and that sigh of his articulates our own desires: "Oh that I had wings like a dove, that I might fly away and be at rest!"

What the soul wants is some unrelaxing, all-propelling, motive; some strong and working force, which shall press it against the backward setting currents, and urge it onward in the face of difficulty and danger and through hindrance.

I have found a marvelous statement of such motive power in Paul's first Epistle to the Corinthians. These Corinthians to whom Paul wrote were erring brethren. They had become defiled with the heathenism of their bad city; they were tolerating and excusing heinous sin. They had left fighting the devil to contend with each other. They were manufacturing scandal for religion. Paul, coming to the rescue, plants among them the controlling motive for the Christian life. That must hold them. That must compel them. That must unite them. That must purify them. That, or nothing can. But that can, that will, that does.

"Now I beseech you, brethren, *by the name of* our Lord Jesus Christ." The name of Christ means Christ himself; his person, his work, his love. What he is, his name stands for.

This, then, is the motive force for the Christian life—the name Christ Jesus; or, to put it into words a little more usual to our lips: I beseech you, therefore, brethren, *for the sake of* our Lord Jesus Christ.

CHARACTER AND TRIAL.

IF real triumph ever come to anybody, it will be reached through character, and in no other way. Water rises to its level, and no higher. In the sight of God; and in the long run, in the sight of man, too, for that matter,— we strike the measure-point of our essential being; we rise as loftily as we are.

But now such triumphant character must be schooled and educated by trial. I know not where this fact is better shown than in the history of Joseph.

I am quite sure that any casual reader of these old Scriptures would be very apt to too much cushion and glove the imprisonment in which Joseph found himself caught and gripped.

Turn to the 105th Psalm. Speaking of God's care of his Hebrew people, as illustrated in their early history, the Psalmist says: "He sent a man before them, even Joseph, who was sold for a servant, whose feet they hurt with fetters; he was laid in iron. Until the time that his word came, the word of the Lord tried him." Or, to bring out the meaning by a translation nearer to the original, "He sent before them a man. Sold for a slave was Joseph. They hurt with a fetter his feet; into iron came his soul, until the time that his word came to pass. The saying of Jehovah tried him."

> Stone walls do not a prison make,
> Nor iron bars a cage.

John Bunyan can find celestial visions even in his Bedford jail, and Madame Guyon can take sweet refuge in the heart of the Crucified, behind the bars which shut her in, and Joseph can be free in mind though he be chained in body. But I think we must all confess that Bedford Jail and French prisons and Egyptian dungeons are not very pleasant places, and that these verses from this Psalm, showing us Joseph fettered till the manacles cut his flesh, and his soul closed about with iron, do show us Jehovah subjecting his servant to a very severe and consuming trial. Think of some of the elements of Joseph's trial. There was an "Arab strain of blood and habit" in these earlier Israelites. They were wont to wander at their own sweet wills. They were not even held by houses, as we are. Their tents could be swiftly pitched and as swiftly moved. They were accustomed to the breadth of the Syrian plain, and to the freedom of the Syrian mountain. A caged canary bird does not give you such feeling of restraint as does a caged eagle. I shall never forget the look of dejection I used to see upon the face of a captive Indian in the far West. It did not seem as though he of the plain and of the mountain ought to be confined. Joseph belonged to a nationality whose blood was Arab, and whose vocation was the shepherd's. A dungeon was a poor exchange for the sweeping uplands of Judea, and for the snowy shoulders of Hermon. He was at the age, too, when physical freedom is most precious, and physical bondage most intolerable. Here was one element of the iron into which his soul came.

Notice another element which must have made his bondage bitter. He could not feel that he deserved it. He had done nothing which could warrant such strange treatment. It was the murderous hatred and jealousy of his brothers which had hung him with a slave's chains, and so had been the primary cause of his present plight. If a man has been really wrong, and has been caught in the rightful doom of wrong, there may be even a slight peace and satisfaction in the consciousness that he suffers rightly. But such poor solace even was denied Joseph. He did not suffer rightly in any way, at least upon the human side.

Think of another element in the iron which gripped his soul. The very hardest thing to endure in the wide world is the result of wrong when you have really done the right. When a man has called on God, and summoned his energy, and struck against temptation, and smitten it down, then for him to get the punishment which had belonged to him had he yielded, then to have burned into him the stigma of the very wickedness he had spurned—that is iron the most wounding and tearing for anybody's soul. Where, then, is God, the just and the judging? It is here that the blackest despair flings down its horrid pall. It is here that the wildest and most tormenting doubt asks its bewildering questions. It is here that the iron cuts away the strongest sinews of a noble purpose. If when I do in God's sight, what in my deepest soul I know God would have me; if I have dashed aside the evil thing; if I have refused to do the wickedness because I could not sin against God; and if then God does not stand by me; and lets the foulness smutch me when I have really kept my garments white; and lets the doom smite me which should have smitten had I fallen into the vileness,—why then God has forgotten, or God does not care, or God is cruel. The foundations are destroyed, and "what can the righteous do?" Fetters which hurt the feet are nothing to this fetter, whose sharp edges cut the soul. Like Cain, we cry; and just because we have not been Cain-like is our cry the bitterer, and the more despairing: "My punishment is greater than I can bear."

It was such barbed iron as this which entered the soul of Joseph. He had battled with temptation and had triumphed; but it all turned out as if he had groveled in a foul defeat.

I do not say that you are to meet trials so terrific and so consuming as those of Joseph, if you are to be lifted into the triumph of a holy character. But I do say this—that as trial lay in the path of Joseph, so trial of some sort must lie in yours. You cannot see the real gleam in the diamond, except you cut and polish it. Its preciousness depends upon the cutting. What now shall be said for the comfort of the diamond amid its cutting? How shall we vindicate the files, and the whirling, grinding emery-wheel? Shall we say to it, that being cut it shall stand in gorgeous setting, that it shall be worn as some rare pendant, that it shall glisten in some crown? You shall be set better, being ground, O diamond, than you were set before you endured the grinding. Is that all we have got to say?

Or, to come back to Joseph, is this all we have to tell him,—"O Joseph, you are having hard times now, but you shall get into better times at last. Your fetters will fall off, your prison gates will open, you shall reach up into compensations; instead of slave, you shall become a prince."

I think Joseph, and any other earnest-minded man would have right to answer: "That is the meanest and poorest sort of comfort. Am I a child, that I should take an undeserved whipping, and then be afterwards comforted with sugar-plums? If there be no real reason for my horrible imprisonment, and for its barbed iron that has been cutting my soul through, then your attempt to comfort is gall instead of balm, because it robs me of my soul's most stalwart stay—that God is just and loving, and really on the side of those who fear and honor him. What I want, more than princely thrones and pleasant times, is to be sure that God is; and that he is no capricious despot, but a kind and wise and just and loving Father. This I must be sure of, whether I be prisoner or prince. This I must be sure of, or else my soul is the captive of despair.

Now, there is such righteous reason for Joseph, and for you and me, amid our trials, and that reason is to be found in God's determination to lift us into noble character. You grind the diamonds, not, primarily, that you may set them well, but that you may let out their lustrous gleam. God grinds souls that he may fill them with the light of true, pure character. That was the reason for Joseph's trial, that is the reason for yours and mine.

Very different from the soft, effeminate, tale-telling, unwise young man was the calm, grand, sympathetic, self-controlling, nobly forgiving prince. Between the two, God had been working with the iron of trial.

THE BEST LAST.

THE exclamation of the governor of the feast at the wedding in Cana is suggestive of a great principle.

"Every man at the beginning doth set forth good wine, and when men have well drunk"— that is, when satiety has begun to come, and the pleasurable and discerning sense has slackened— "then that which is worse; but thou hast kept the good wine until now," the governor said.

And herein is disclosed a constant principle concerning the gifts of Christ. This glory streams from him—that what he gives does not pall and fail, does not perish with the using, does not grow from more to less, but grows from less to more. Evermore Christ's last is best.

Just at this time there was a man living who had the whole world in his control. To him, as to a greedy centre, were flowing constantly the fairest, choicest things the world could give. For him the most precious vintage. For him the rarest luxuries of earth and sea and various climates.

A little after this, that he might lay off all care, and meet no hindrance as he fed himself with all voluptuous pleasures, he withdrew to an island, soft with the tenderest sunshine, and delicious with enchanting shade, and fascinating with smooth verdure and swelling hill—the island of Capreae, set there like an emerald amid the sapphire waters of the Bay of Naples. He tried, perhaps, the hugest experiment ever tried as to the real and continued satisfaction of the world's best wine.

"*Tristissimus ut constat hominum*"—it is confessed the most gloomy of mankind, says Pliny of him. And from amidst his splendid experiment with the world's wine; from his wealth inestimable; from his freedom from care; from his green bowers of pleasantness; from his palaces, the richest that the world could build; from his utterly ungirded and Titanic self-indulgence—the wretched Tiberius, the Emperor of all the world, can only send out this wail to the Roman Senate: "May all the gods and goddesses destroy me worse than I daily feel if I know, Conscript Fathers, what to write to you."

Ah! the world's wine palls. There is an adder in its cup. It stings with remorse. It blights with the shadow of coming and certain doom.

See Paul, victor though defeated, triumphing under the very gleam of Nero's sword: "I have fought a good fight, I have finished my course, I have kept the faith, henceforth there is laid up for me a crown of righteousness."

See John Wesley, with the rapturous smile upon his face, saying, with dying breath: "The best of all is, God is with us."

Hear the Christian Bishop Janes, settled firmly, for a life long, on the Rock of Ages, sounding forth this as his dying testimony: "I am not disappointed."

"And the twelve gates were twelve pearls;

every several gate was of one pearl; and the street of the city was pure gold, as it were transparent glass." "And God shall wipe away all tears from their eyes; and there shall be no more death, neither sorrow nor crying, neither shall there be any more pain, for the former things are passed away."

That city may be ours, if we will have it so; if we will but give ourselves by faith to Christ. For us shall swing inward those gates of pearl; the gold, as it were transparent glass, shall be pavement for our feet; for us all tears shall be wiped away, and death be vanquished, and sorrow be helpless to scale the jeweled walls protecting us, and pain shall never pierce us more. And then, how true it will be, what better language for our lips than this, "Master, thou hast kept the good wine until now."

FAITH.

IN order that Christ may do anything for a man, he everywhere prescribes an absolutely necessary condition. This condition is faith. Christ always says: "If you would be saved by me, you must believe me."

The Scripture is very explicit on this point. He that *believeth* shall have everlasting life. "God so loved the world that he gave his only begotten Son, that whosoever *believeth* on him should not perish, but have everlasting life." "He that *believeth* on me, though he were dead, yet shall he live." "These things are written that ye might *believe* that Jesus is the Christ, the Son of God, and that, believing, ye might have life through his name." Everywhere, between man's lostness and Christ's rescue, between man's guiltiness and Christ's forgiveness, between man's death and Christ's life, stands, as the bridge connecting them, this indispensable thing, faith.

And, if you will look into the life of Christ, you will find that, while he stood among men like a fountain in the desert, eager to let forth the healing waters that were in him, to fill their thirst and ease their pain and soothe their sorrow, he was always most particular to fix between himself and those he loved this channel and connection of faith. We read that in one place he could not do many mighty works because of their unbelief. Before he put forth any special wonders, how often he looked on the hearts about him, to see if there were in them this aptitude and condition for his help! The unloosing of his power seemed to depend on this. Sometimes he would wake up this faith by a question, as if to fix the thought, as to blind Bartimeus: "What wilt thou that I should do unto thee?" Sometimes it was by some hidden, searching requirement, bringing to light any hidden reservation of soul which prevented faith, as when he said to the young man: "Go, sell what thou hast and give to the poor, and come and follow me." When the leper, muffled in his sackcloth, stood before him, saying, "Lord, if thou wilt, thou canst make me clean," his faith at once called forth the healing word and touch of Christ. When the centurion was sure that a word of Christ's, at a distance from his sick servant, was as powerful a thing as the presence of Christ by his sick servant's side, he healed his servant by a word, exclaiming: "I have not found so great faith; no, not in Israel." When the Syro-Phœnician woman came pleading for her demon-possessed daughter, he did not answer her at once. He proved her first. He seemed to thrust hard obstacle into the pleading face of prayer. "It is not meet to take the children's bread and cast it unto the dogs." Yet, when she had the faith which would cling to him, notwithstanding all discouragement, and would plead her lowly suit, "Yea, Lord, but the dogs eat of the crumbs which fall from their master's table," then faith won blessing, and he dismissed her with the joy of her healed daughter in her heart, and with this benediction on her: "O woman, great is thy faith. Be it unto thee even as thou wilt."

So always between all that Christ can do and longs to do for men and the men themselves, rises this inevitable and rocky condition, faith.

Why, then, is it so necessary that from the hearts of men toward Christ there must come forth this faith before Christ can in anywise help them? This is the reason: faith is the appropriating faculty. The curriculum of a college will do the student no good whatever, except, by personal appropriation, he take hold of it. The man overboard will drown, though the life-buoy flung from the ship's deck float within his reach, if he do not put forth his hand and seize it. In the Old Economy, the law said: "And he [the offerer] shall put [lean] his hand upon the head of the burnt offering, and it shall be accepted for him to make atonement for him." Before, even amid those shadows, the shadow could change to the least substance, the man must confess everything as his, and for the sake of his sin. As another has somewhere said: "If any Israelite had said to his servant, I have done something wrong, something that requires an offering. I am very busy just now; do you take a lamb to the priest, and let him make an atonement for me—in such a case there would have been no acceptance, no blessing." The priest would have told the servant that such proxy religion could not be permitted. So, in the New Economy, there must be a personal appropriation. The man must lean the hand of his faith upon the Lord Christ, before he can receive from Christ the help and healing that are in him. Faith is the appropriating faculty.

But now it is not necessary that our faith be such jubilant faith as that of Paul, when he flung forth the challenge, "Who shall lay anything to the charge of God's elect?" nor such confident faith as that of Paul again, when he said: "I can do all things through Christ which strengtheneth me;" nor such victorious faith as that of Paul again, when he said: "I am now ready to be offered. Henceforth, there is laid up for me a crown of righteousness." It is not necessary that our faith be so fixed, so firm, so large, so perfect, before it can become the channel through which shall flow to us the grace and peace and blessing of the loving Christ. John Bunyan has a character called Mr. Fearing, who yet made triumphant entrance into the Celestial City; and there be many Feeble Faiths and Mr. Fearings among the pilgrims now, who take hold of Christ with a faith most small and weak, but who yet do take hold of him by faith, and into whom, therefore, his salvation flows.

That woman who dared do no more than lay her finger on the fringe of the Master's garment, is an instance of a faith by no means intelligent and strong, but still of a faith sufficient to bring her into contact with the helping and the healing Christ.

Faith includes these two elements: First, loss of trust in self. Second, dependence of trust on another. Take a child by way of illustration. A child-life is always a life of faith. That little child — what can it do for itself? It cannot find its way through the city street; yet it does not fear. It cannot find its clothing, or make its clothing, or clothe itself; yet it has no fear of nakedness. It cannot build a house or buy a bed; yet it does not fear that it will be shelterless or without a pillow. It cannot grow a harvest or manufacture food; yet it fears no hunger. It knows its weakness; yet nothing is so certain of care and guidance. No one feels so certain of it, because the parent walks with it on the street; the parent clothes it; the parent builds the house; the parent furnishes and smooths the pillow; the parent gives it bread; and the child, conscious of its own weakness, puts trust in father and in mother, and so is free and glad. That is faith; emptiness of dependence upon self, fullness of dependence on another.

Such faith this woman had. She had lost dependence on herself. The twelve years' sickness and all her money gone to physicians had cured her of self-trust; but this new Rabbi, this great wonder-worker—perhaps the healing in him, which had helped so many others, might help her as well. So, despairing of her own power, tremblingly, almost doubtfully, but yet really, she reaches forth the hand of trust in him and touches him; and thus this tie of faith was formed between herself and the healing Christ, and thus the vigor which was in her Lord became her own.

Christ respects a man's free volition. Faith is that movement of the soul through which it passes into surrender to him and seizure of him. Faith is the appropriating faculty. Without faith, nothing in religion is possible; with faith, everything is possible, because by faith the soul allows the incoming and the energy of the saving Christ.

PRAYER.

"MAKING mention of you in my prayers," says Paul to the Ephesians. A great sight these words reveal—Paul at prayer. And right here we come at a reason for Paul's vast and various success. Paul not only wrought much. *Paul prayed much.*

Heed the lesson. Right here in prayer is to be found the tap-root reason for all high and branching religious achievement in any direction —in the winning of holy character inwardly, in the widening of Christ's kingdom outwardly.

Is there anything more pathetic in all history? He was utterly worn out and very sick. There, as Dr. Blakie tells us, in the vast and tangled wilds of Africa they laid him on a rough bed in the poor hut, his faithful black followers had builded for him, where he spent the night. Next day he lay undisturbed. He asked a few wandering questions about the country. His faithful black followers knew that the end could not be far off. Nothing occurred to attract notice during the early part of the night; but at four in the morning, the black boy who lay at his door called in alarm. By the candle still burning, they saw him, not in bed, but kneeling at the bedside, with his head buried in his hands upon the pillow. He had passed away on the furthest of all his journeys, and without a single attendant. But he had died in the act of prayer—prayer, offered in that reverential attitude about which he was always so particular; commending his own spirit, with all his dear ones, as was his wont, into the hands of his Saviour; and commending Africa, with all her woes and sins and wrongs, to the Avenger of the oppressed and the Redeemer of the lost.

And here again you come at the reason of a life like David Livingstone's—so pure and strong in itself, so vast in beneficent result. Livingstone made mention of Africa in his prayers; he died doing it; so, though he died, he was victor of her.

Prayer was the beating heart of so great a life.

Or, go further back and think of that critical moment pregnant with your liberties and mine, with the free civilization of these latter days, when, in the presence of the Emperor Charles V., the master of half the world, and of his glittering court, and of the scarlet emissaries of a grasping and tyrannizing Romanism throwing as yet unbroken and blighting shadow over Europe— the monk Luther, at the Diet of Worms, was given grace to stand for the plain truths of that Bible which Rome had shoved out of the hands and memories of men; when, notwithstanding crowned Emperor and powerful state, and apostate and oppressive church, he was given grace to speak those words which meant an unfettered Bible, and so free thought, and so your liberties and mine—"Here I stand; I can do no otherwise; God help me; Amen." There were no braver, more far-reaching words ever said by human lips since the morning stars sang together.

But the reason for grace to say them, is to be found in Luther's prayers before he said them.

Listen while one, overhearing while he prays, takes the passionate pleadings down—

"O Almighty Eternal God! what a thing is this world! How do the people speak against thee! How little is their confidence in God! How weak and tender is the flesh; how strong and busy the devil, with his apostles and worldly wise men, who only look at what is great and mighty and has a lofty appearance.

"If I should turn my eyes that way, all would be over with me. Ah God, O my God, stand by me! O my God, help me against all the wisdom and reason of this world! Do it thou; for thou canst do it, thou alone. It is thy cause; it is not mine. Come, O my God. I am ready. I will go like a little lamb, for the cause is just and is thine."

The prayers of Luther made his words half battles. Because by prayer he took hold of the arm of Strength, he was strong.

Or, see the Apostle Paul kneeling in his

imprisonment, and making mention of these Ephesians in his prayers; and not of these Ephesians only, but of the Corinthians and the Colossians and Philippians and the Thessalonians and of Timothy and Philemon. Read his Epistles, and you will see how constant was his habit of bringing his own needs, like his thorn in the flesh, and the needs of all the churches, before his God in prayer. You may find what reasons you please for Paul's vast success in the great duty of his apostleship; because he was learned; because he was naturally so active and so enthusiastic; because while a Jew, and great in their culture, he was also deeply conversant with Greek culture, and so among the Jews could become as a Jew, and among the Greeks as a Greek. But while all these are reasons, and without doubt exerted mighty influence, they would all have been as nothing without *the* reason; Paul prayed. He took hold of the strength of God by prayer. He girded himself with that great strength by prayer. He made alliance with God by prayer.

Let us heed the lesson. Christ said, "Without me ye can do nothing," and therefore without prayer we can do nothing, for it is by prayer we take hold of Christ.

Hear John Knox as he cries, "Give me Scotland or I die." Hear Zwingli, the Swiss Reformer, as in prayer he grips the word of Christ, "Hast thou not promised to be with us unto the end of the world!" Hear Melanchthon, Luther's friend and helper, as he says, "Prayer is the best means of consolation; thus trouble impels me to prayer, and prayer drives away trouble." Hear Philip Henry tell his children, "Be sure you look to your secret duty; keep up that, whatever you do; the soul cannot prosper in the neglect of it; apostasy generally begins at the closet door." Hear Samuel Rutherford as he tells of a special place in which he was wont to pray, "There I wrestled with the angel and prevailed. Woods, trees, meadows, and hills are my witnesses." Hear Jonathan Edwards, as at the beginning of his religious life, he resolves "Very much to exercise myself in prayer all my life long." Hear Robert McCheyne say, "I am persuaded that I ought never to do anything without prayer, and, if possible, special secret prayer." Hear Dr. Arnold, of Rugby, tell his pupils that he intended to offer a prayer before the first lesson, that the day's work might be undertaken and carried on solely to the glory of God and their own improvement, that he might be the better enabled to do his work. Remember Harlan Page, as he "expected success from God through the blessing of the Holy Spirit in answer to prayer." And as these, and such as these, followed Paul in making mention of their needs in prayer, let us do likewise. Neither as men and women in the hurry and bustle of the daily life, nor as a church, nor as preaching in a pulpit, nor as teaching a Sunday-school class, nor as sowing the seed of the kingdom along the wayside, nor as engaged in bringing up our children, nor as set in any of life's relations, nor as burdened with any of life's duties, can we either be what we ought, or do what we ought, without prayer.

More things are wrought by prayer
Than this world dreams of. · Wherefore let
         Thy voice
Rise like a fountain for me night and day;
For what are men better than sheep or goats
That nourish a blind life within the brain
If, knowing God, they lift not hands of
         Prayer
Both for themselves and those who call them friend?
For so the whole round world is every way
Bound by gold chains about the feet of God.

PRAYER AND FAITH.

THE elder Pliny was a great philosopher. He was as fine a specimen of a man as heathenism produced. He was much given to the study of nature, chiefly that he might gain some hint concerning the Immeasurable Creative Spirit whom he believed to be behind and through it. But, as I have read of him, he has seemed to me oppressed always with a great sadness;—life to him was little illumined. He was restless with longing; stricken with the famine of the soul. No man's appreciation could be more profound of the exalted Spirit of the universe. But, as he looked at nature and thought of the dim Creator, he saw nothing to bridge the chasm between man and that Unknown, All Transcendent Spirit. And so, shut away from the light of any special revelation, he came to look at the world only as some mighty mechanism tyrannized over by destiny, overbuilt by a brazen sky, concerning which no thought ruffled the expanse of the Supreme Intelligence.

"What God is," he says, "if indeed he be anything distinct from the world, it is beyond the compass of man's understanding to know. But it is a foolish delusion which has sprung from human weakness and human pride to imagine that such an Infinite Spirit would concern himself with the petty affairs of men."

That was the secret of his sadness. How great soever and self-contained a man may be, he cannot carry a hopeful and joyful heart if he believes that God does not care for him; and that one cannot reach, touch, move his God.

There are many men just now, writing upon the lids of the Bible "Antiquated," "Useless," "Outgrown," discarding all revelation but their own doubtful interpretations of scientific facts, who re-assert this old belief of Pliny's, and seek to spread again over the world the ancient heathen gloom.

But the Bible comes to men expressly to scatter such sadness. The burden of its revelations is that God does care; can somehow be touched with the feelings of their infirmities; can be moved to listen to their cry; and answer their requests. "Like as a father pitieth his children, so the Lord pitieth them that fear him."

"I waited patiently for the Lord, and he inclined unto me and heard my cry." "When thou passest through the waters I will be with thee. When thou walkest through fire thou shalt not be burned, neither shall the flame kindle upon thee nor any heat, for I am the Lord thy God, the Holy One of Israel, thy Saviour." "The Lord is nigh unto all them that call upon him, to all them that call upon him in truth."

But not only does God tell us thus in words that he is sensitive to human want; he has written out the same truth in the distinctive characters of action. Christ, the express image of the God-head bodily, left heaven and came to earth to let men know the Infinite Father's heart. You remember how it was. There was never a prayer uttering toward Jesus, the least pleading, that the face of Jesus did not brighten back in answer to it. The heart of Jesus is the heart of God.

But not only is it thus revealed to us that God cares for us and can be moved by us; but we are also told by what force we may thus reach him. That force, the Scripture tells us over and over again, is faith. "He that cometh to God must believe that he is, and that he is the Rewarder of them that diligently seek him." "Without faith it is impossible to please God." Faith reaches up its hand and takes hold on God. Faith touches the heart of God. Faith moves the arm that moves the world. God will say to faith, "Be it unto thee even as thou wilt."

The trouble is that many think themselves to hold faith toward God who really have but certain opinions about him. Faith is never a mere opinion. Here, for instance, is a man who will repeat the creed for you glibly—he is not an

Atheist. When you tell him that God is loving and heedful of his creatures, he does not dissent; and yet this man never tests in any personal, real way the love and care of God. He never comes into contact with God, nor does he care to. He sees the truth of an interfering God as men see mountains on the remote limits of the horizon, dim with the distance, shrouded—almost concealed—with mists. Such thought toward God is never faith; it is opinion only. It holds no real relation to the management of life. It never becomes an energetic element in spiritual pulsations. But faith which reaches out and touches God is not alone assent of the intellect, it is consent of the heart. It believes in God, and *embarks on the belief,* as men give themselves to ships with which to cross the ocean. It conceives of God as full of love and minute in care; and boldly goes into his presence to claim his love and task his care. It stands before the divine promises as soldiers before some fort, sure that they can win possession of it. It takes God at his word and grandly holds him to his word.

This is faith. Clear assent of the intellect and passionate consent of the heart. It is not opinion; it is belief clothed in the flesh and blood of action.

When prayers miss such faith as this, they are like men paralyzed. They have no moving power.

It was Wesley's constant prayer that he might have more faith. It should be ours as well! Thus, as an old writer has it, "our prayers will not come limping home."

FAITH AND RESULTS.

I HEARD, some time ago, a little incident which has since helped me mightily. One of Mr. Spurgeon's preachers was discouraged. He seemed to be effecting nothing. He came to tell his discouragement. He said:

"Mr. Spurgeon, I have been preaching and preaching, and it does apparently no good whatever."

In his quick way, Mr. Spurgeon immediately answered:

"Well, you do not believe that God will bless every truth that you declare, do you?"

"Oh, certainly not," answered the discouraged man.

"And that is just the reason why he does not," solemnly replied the great London victor for the gospel.

The trouble was, the preacher had been going

at his duty faithlessly, and so had reaped nothing. He did not believingly expect, therefore he did not achieve.

I heard the other day an incident in the same direction, which, strange as it may seem, is still strictly true. In New York, a young woman became much concerned for the religious welfare of her brother. He was a non-church-goer. It seemed impossible to induce him within the gospel proclamation. One Lord's Day morning, much burdened for him, she determined believingly to pray that that day he might attend the services in her own church. She asked the Lord for the gift of his attendance, and then, relying on the promise that those who believe receive, set about believing that the gift that day requested would be that day granted. At the breakfast table her faith met its first assault. When she asked her brother if he would not attend church with her that day, he replied:

"I cannot; I must go to Brooklyn."

Still she held on believingly; went to her Sunday-school class, praying and believing;

entered the church, praying and believing. The services began. Her brother did not appear. The time wore on until the sermon was just commencing. Then, thinking faith useless longer, she deliberately gave up believing. And so the worship was concluded, and she went home.

Reaching home, she found her brother there, and was at once greeted with the remark:

"I almost came to your church this morning. I went over to Brooklyn, but somehow thought I would come back. At about eleven I reached the corner near your church, determining to go in. Then I thought it too late, and did not enter."

When the sister ceased believing, *at that moment* the brother stopped on his way toward the literal answer of her prayer.

Now just what the relation may be between our faith and definite answer to our prayer; between our faith and triumphant religious results,—we may not be able to tell precisely. Heavy mists hang here, which the keenest eye of our human reason cannot pierce. But that there is *some* relation, real and radical, is the constant assertion of the Scriptures: "According to your faith be it unto you."

The Christian harvester who does not go forth expecting to reap a harvest with the sickle of God's truth will surely gather no grain. The trouble with the most of us is we do not believe enough, we do not expect enough. What we need is faith which grips the promise unrelaxingly. It is he who, like William Carey, believes great things of God, and, therefore, expects great things from him, who shall master obstacles, and plant the standard of the cross upon the battlements of sin.

One of the best ways I know in which faith may reverently put God to the test is the Inquiry Room. After the sermon, or after the teaching of the Sunday-school lesson, give, somehow, chance for quiet, personal religious conversation. It is quite surprising how thus immediate results of religious effort will appear. We are helpless, but the Holy Spirit is Almighty. That Almightiness is pledged to us. Let us believe the divine pledging, and act as though we did. Let us go forth in a faithful expectancy. David says, "My voice shalt thou hear in the morning, O Lord; in the morning will I direct my prayer unto thee, and will look up." It ought to be translated, *and will look out.* That is to say, David declares he will believingly expect answer to his prayer, and keep his eye open that he may see the answer coming. It is a principle we should never forget in our Christian working, that results do really spring from energetic and persistent faith.

DOUBT.

JOHN the Baptist, doubting in his prison, and sending to Christ to ask, "Art thou he that should come, or do we look for another?" is a most suggestive sight. It is helpful, too, since a "fellow-feeling makes us wondrous kind." If doubt smote the sturdy Baptist, it is not wonderful that now and then it smites ourselves. Some of the reasons for John's doubt may be suggestive of the reasons for our own.

One reason plainly was a misconception of the divine way and time. John had been preaching the kingdom of heaven as at hand. The kingdom of heaven—what does that mean? It means right triumphant, the evil crushed, bad men undermost, good men uppermost. And he who was to be King over this kingdom, and who was to lead it in, had come at last. John had heard the voice from heaven approve him, and had himself welcomed him to his great mission. Why, then, should not the kingdom come at once? This was the time for it, there was the King for it. Now the divine fire was to scathe and burn. Now, with fan in hand, the Mighty One was to purge the world's threshing floor, was to gather the wheat into his garner, was to consume the chaff.

But as John looked out from that prison of Machærus, he could see no signs of righteous victory. He could see no attempt on the part of Jesus to win it. The skies were just as blue as ever. The earth was just as firm. The processes of providence were just as calm. He whom John thought to be King was only preaching to the poorer classes, was only healing here and there a few sick, was tarrying at wedding feasts, was dining with Pharisees and publicans. Herod still sat secure upon his throne. His crime flaunted itself. The partner of his guilt was triumphant in her royalty so foully gained. Evil had the upper hand. John himself pined in prison. And yonder was the Messiah, only a poor Jewish peasant after all, wearing no crown, not even seeking to be crowned. If the kingdom were to come, why did it not come? Where was the heavenly reign; where was the Holy Ghost, where was the fire, where were the earthquake and the whirlwind?

So doubts began to gnaw away John's faith. Perhaps he had made a mistake; perhaps this Jesus was not, after all, the Messiah. Wherever John looked, he began to see only this misty, wavering, intangible, tormenting, horrible Perhaps.

But John's trouble was the thinking that God's kingdom must come in John's way, not in God's; that God's kingdom must come in John's time, not in God's.

And is not this a frequent reason for our doubt to-day? We forget that God's ways are not ours, nor his time ours. If we cannot see the feet of God treading that path which our thoughts mark out, if we cannot see the hand of God disclosing itself in that time which we have called a crisis—then God has no kingdom, then the universe stands draped and dreary in the fog of a terrible Perhaps.

And yet, O imprisoned preacher, O forerunner of Messiah, the kingdom of God has come and its King has appeared! The kingdom has been set up. That King shall reign—not swiftly, suddenly, with vengeance, with fire, as you think; but slowly, patiently, through suffering, the cross, the death, yet, oh how surely and gloriously as God thinks!

In the old time in Connecticut, they had what was called the Standing Order—an ecclesiastical arrangement, a kind of union of Church and State, fraught with all sorts of evil, and directly opposed to the spirit of our free institutions. Old Dr. Lyman Beecher was Pastor in Litchfield, belonged to the Congregational Standing Order, believed in the system utterly, and when measures were taken to overthrow it, fought them with his whole strength. But he was defeated, and then Dr. Beecher thought that the foundations of the universe were out of course. But he lived long enough to see that what he had thought destruction, was really God's upbuilding, and long afterward he said about that time: "For several days I suffered what no tongue can tell for *the best thing that ever happened to the State of Connecticut.*" Ah, we want more faith in God, and less in our own rickety human methods.

Also John was now a prisoner. Here was another cause for doubt. It was one thing to be the commanding preacher of the Wilderness, under the bright heavens, fanned by the free air. It was another thing to be in prison and chained to waiting.

Well, sometimes there are for us prisons— prisons of *inactivity*. John, struggling and preaching in the Wilderness, needed no proof that the Christ had come. John, shut up in the prison, fell into doubt. As bats gather in dark caves, so do doubts spread their hideous wings in these glooms of inactivity. Perhaps we cannot explain it, but it is a law of life which experience declares, that action and certainty go together. A man full of work has no time to doubt, he has only time to do. A man who has nothing to do but to sit theorizing and sentimentalizing with himself, will soon find that he will have enough to do in fighting doubt. In this working world, where the Father worketh hitherto and the Son works, where the seasons turn their ceaseless round, where buds expand to leaves, and flowers to bloom, and seeds press into harvests, things will always seem awry to a man out of sympathy and community with the universal energy. A great reason why men are such large doubters religiously, is because they are such small doers religiously.

There is the prison of *ill health*. I have seen those who were the sweetest saints of God, very pale and sad with confinement here. A man in health is like a broad and roomy house, standing upon the hill-top, upon all sides of which the sun pours healthful light, and in all sides of which the open doors and lighted windows receive the radiance, and the breezes, and the perfume. A man in sickness is like that house built into some close city block, with the doors shut, with the windows narrowed and fastened down, damp and darkened. What can a man know of the glory of the spring in such a house? So is it that sickness sometimes fastens the doors and walls up the windows of the senses, and puts the soul in prison. In that darkness, doubt is very apt to dwell.

There is the prison of conscious *sinning*. Said a man to me: "I cannot pray and do this thing; I cannot indulge in this and go to God." Of course he could not. He had shut himself within the prison of sinfulness. He had barred out the light altogether. God could not be near him; and where God is not, all fears must be. The man who sins willfully cannot help doubting deeply. Doubtless, there was no such cause for the doubt of John; but it is a frequent cause for doubt with us.

But John took the right step out of doubt. He gave himself to prayer. "Now when John had heard in the prison the words of Christ, he sent two of his disciples and said unto him, 'Art thou he that should come, or do we look for another?'" That is the worst possible thing to do with doubt—to hold it within yourself, to brood over it, to wonder how a man who has once been certain can now be so uncertain, to question back and forth whether a man who has so little faith can ever reach up into firmer. Christ would have you trust him as you would your friend. If you are bound into friendship with another, and something comes that casts a shadow on it—your friend does something or says something, or you hear that he has done or said something, which clashes with his profession of love to you—then, if you love him, you will not take that thing which makes you doubt him, and harbor it, and dwell upon it, and revolve it, but you will go to him at once in the noble frankness of friendship, and ask for explanation. So treat Christ. Tell him your doubt in prayer, and he shall meet you as kindly as he met the doubting cry of John.

Only remember that, while John could not free himself from his prison, it is sometimes possible for you to free yourself from yours.

For you have shut yourself in, you have not been shut in. A real prayer means the casting down of such prison walls as willfully thrust themselves between your soul and the vision of Christ's face.

RESOURCES.

I SPENT a lovely summer day at Malmaison. It is about seven miles west of Paris. The palace was sadly shattered when I saw it. It had received no repair from Prussian shells; but as I passed through its rooms and wandered along the lovely avenues of its sweet grounds, and loitered by its lake-sides, I seemed to be attended by the presence of those who rendered it historic—of him beneath whose tread Europe was wont to tremble—of her, the wedded and the wronged, the gentle and the suffering Josephine.

It was when his wonderful star flamed brightest, and before the shadow of that disastrous wrong had smitten her, that Malmaison was most his home. But there was one place in which I waited longest. It was a summer house, apart from the main chateau; set by itself amid a tangle of shading trees. In the centre of its single room there stood a large and level table. Down upon you from the walls there shone the great glittering N., and underneath were written in golden letters the names of his signal victories. This summer-house was the study of the great man. It was in this room he elaborated the plans of many of his most marvelous campaigns. It was upon that table that his maps were spread and studied. It was within these walls that he calculated and arranged his resources of men, material, money. It was because he was so strong in various resources, conceived and marshaled here, that he was so strong for victory in a hundred fights. The meanest soldier marching beneath his banners went as in certain triumph, because he knew that the great Napoleon had laid his mighty thought and hand upon mighty and multitudinous resources, and that since he was his soldier he would surely win.

Lift now your thoughts to another Captain, and to an infinitely grander conflict. Said a British statesman, "A great nation cannot have a little war." It is no little war that Christianity

11*

is waging. In the words of the now classic sermon of Dr. Wayland, " Its object will not have been accomplished till every idol temple shall be utterly abolished, and a temple of Jehovah erected in its room. Until this earth, instead of being a theatre, on which mortal beings are preparing by crime for eternal condemnation, shall become one universal temple, in which the children of men are learning the anthems of the blessed above, and becoming meet to join the general assembly and church of the first-born whose names are written in heaven."

Now, the question is one of resources. What is there in Christianity which can make the world capitulate?

The battle had been already joined. The crash of conflict was already sounding. Nero was desolating the faithful by fire and by sword. It was a crisis. There were to be other crises still. John is wrenched from the Church at Ephesus, and flung a prisoner upon that lonely rock which breaks the waves of the Egæan Sea. Then for his comfort, and for the comfort and courage of all Christians, there was flashed upon him the vast vision of the Revelation. It casts its shining circle around the succeeding ages. Affliction there shall be. Seals shall be broken, and trumpets shall resound. There shall be flying angels and falling stars, and signs in the sun and moon and earth. There shall be heresies and schisms. There shall be gatherings of opposing forces, and Armageddon contests. But the Great Captain shall go steadily from conquering to conquering. Never shall he be worsted. Till at last, as tempests pass into the softest calm, the vision ends in the new heaven and the new earth, wherein dwelleth righteousness—in the tabernacle of God with men—in the tearlessness, the deathlessness, and the painlessness of the redeemed; for the former things are passed away.

Now, in almost the first sentence of this prophecy of triumph, I find a statement of the resources of Christianity. John received his message from Jesus Christ, who is the faithful Witness, the First-begotten of the dead the

Prince of the kings of the earth — he that hath loved us and washed us from our sins in his own blood. Here are the Christ's resources. Marching with him, they are ours. These must out-measure the puissance of any foe. Analyze a moment these resources.

First, the truth. The message comes from Jesus Christ, who is the faithful Witness. A faithful witness is one who utters the exact truth, and truth is something conquering and eternal in its very nature.

Second, the truth substantiated. He who is the faithful Witness is the *First-begotten of the dead.* The indestructible fact of the Resurrection is the primal sanction for every declaration of our Christianity.

Third, present divine power. For that ever faithful Witness, and the First-begotten of the dead, is now the *Prince of the kings of the earth.* In another place, the apostle calls him "the King of the ages." The pierced hand is on the helm of things.

Fourth. Another resource of Christianity is

sacrificial love. "Unto him that loved us, and washed us from our sins in his own blood." The fervor of the broken heart of the Lord Christ must melt all worldly opposition at the last.

Let us, tired pastor, wavering Sunday-school teacher, wearied worker for righteousness anywhere, be courageous, then, and hopeful. We are on the winning side of things. The battle may be difficult, but the triumph is certain. Let us fasten our vision upon that, and fight onward even to the death.

WAITING ON THE LORD.

THERE is much speech among us about churches waiting on the Lord. That waiting of the early church before the coming of the Holy Spirit is the best illustration of what such waiting is. If the Lord's churches waited on him more in this fashion, they would certainly become more flooded with his power.

These waited *obediently*. Wondering, not altogether understanding, yet filled with faith, and luminous with an exceeding joy, these disciples come up to Jerusalem, exactly to obey their Lord's command. There they gather in some upper room within the city. The eleven apostles—Peter, James, and John, and those whom the Lord had called with them into apostleship—are there. Mary, the mother of the Lord—she, patient and submissive, saying ever, "Be it unto me according to thy word," she is there. Those who stand in close kinship and brotherhood with Jesus, sharing with Jesus the motherhood of Mary, though not the fatherhood of God,—these, who, at length, believed on him, are there; and those loving women, last at the cross and first at the sepulchre, who had followed him on the sad final journey from Galilee down to Calvary,—these are there; and besides these there is a throng of others whose names we do not know. The whole company of believing, waiting, hoping ones, is one hundred and twenty strong, gathered there together.

Obediently these were waiting; but what was their waiting? A supine, careless, unstrenuous, ineffectual dilly-dallying? Oh, no, that may, indeed, be waiting, but that is never waiting on the Lord.

It was a waiting *grounded on an unquivering faith*. Of the fulfillment of the Lord's promise, they were absolutely sure. The baptism of fire they were certain would descend.

It was a waiting *in continued and energetic prayer*. As the Greek tells us, they intently gave themselves to prayer. Laying hold of the promise of their risen Lord, they pleaded for its fulfillment. Strange, this place which prayer—this intense longing of the human heart, this pleading of the human voice—holds, intermediate, between the promise and the fulfillment of it. And yet it does hold a place so valuable and eminent.

It was a waiting *together*. They were all with one accord in one place. Peter was not absent, because he could not exactly fellowship the previous doubtfulness of Thomas. John was not away, because Peter had once tumbled into a base denial. Mary did not refuse to come, because the Galilean brogue of some of them grated a little on her refinement. None of the men nor any of the women were out of their places, because it was a rainy day, or because it was a sunny day, or because it was not exactly convenient to be there, or because the turban had become a little worn, or the tunic had become a little shabby, or because Andrew or Simon would occupy so much time, or because any were in a cold, listless, careless state. They were waiting together.

And then besides, they were waiting with *one accord*. Their minds and hearts were set utterly, resolutely on this one thing, the fulfillment of the promise, the flaming of the baptism of fire. Perhaps they remembered the word of the Lord Jesus, how he said, "Again I say unto you, that if two of you shall agree on earth as touching anything that they shall ask, it shall be done for them of my Father which is in heaven."

It was a *patient* waiting. Perhaps they thought the baptism of fire would fall on the day succeeding the ascension; if not then, on the day succeeding that. Certainly, then, the day after; but the baptism of fire did not come. Surely, then, when seven days have rolled around, when the full week has elapsed since the ascension; but not then even did the baptism of fire shine. Another day, and then another, and then another still. Ten days have sped away; "not many days" was the promise. But are not these waiting days multiplying to many? Does it not seem as though the shadows were beginning to fall and darken over the fulfillment? And yet they waited obediently, unitedly, accordantly, continuously. They were not disappointed.

If, in these times, we had more of their waiting, I am sure we should receive more of their power.

IDOLIZING.

THAT was a divided family in that old time. Father and mother did not work together. I am afraid there are many people still, like Isaac and Rebecca, married,—and yet not married through and through. Marriage ought to be union of soul, first and foremost. People may live in the same house, and yet they may live in different thoughts. Do you remember that beautiful poem of Bayard Taylor's to his wife:

> I was the crescent; thou
> The silver phantom of the perfect sphere,
> Held in its bosom; in one glory now
> Our lives united shine, and many a year—
> Not the sweet moon of bridal only—we
> One lustre, ever at the full, shall be;
> One pure and rounded light, one planet whole,
> One life developed, one completed soul!
> For I in thee, and thou in me,
> Unite our cloven halves of destiny.

That is a true marriage—where the thoughts

chime, where the purposes are one. Where no division of any sort is in the least permitted; where Isaac will love Jacob for Rebecca's sake, if he cannot for his own, and where Rebecca will love Esau for Isaac's sake, and where both shall plan together the best and most right things for all, without the clash and intrusion of cross purposes. You cannot build the best home upon hearts in any wise divided. It was feared they could not finish Cologne Cathedral, because the foundations were thought to be giving way. You cannot rear the beautiful and heavenward-pointing spires of the finished home unless the foundations of an utter union of heart and purpose in wife and husband are true and strong. Though you may try, there will be sag and breakage somewhere.

Rebecca overhears what Isaac speaks to Esau concerning the giving of the blessing. It will never do to have that purpose consummated. Better than anything else in the world, she loves Jacob. The crown must shine upon his head at any hazard. She will set her mother's

IDOLIZING.

hand to putting it there by fraud, since, as she thinks, there is no other method.

That was idolizing—that affection of Rebecca's, as real precisely as though she had bent before some graven image. It is possible to manufacture idols out of your tenderest and most absorbing loves. Out of the children, even, whom God has given you. And yet, how womanly it all was! There are touches about it you cannot help admiring. How ambitious she was, and yet how self-forgetting! It was of Jacob only she thought, not of herself; how woman-like! It was idolatry of a person, too, rather than of a principle. How woman-like again! As another says: "A man's idolatry is for an idea; a woman's for a person. A man suffers for a monarchy; a woman for a king." She was altogether reckless of the consequences which might come to herself. How like a woman here, too, in the grand devotion of womanhood! When Jacob fears that it will all be found out, and that curse will fall instead of blessing, how womanly and even motherly the answer: "Upon me be thy curse, my son!"

Now, do not make a mistake. A great deal of troubled thought often arises in sensitive hearts lest idols should rise and rule here, in the realm of the affections. I have often heard mothers say, "I love my child so much, I am afraid I make an idol of him." And then they set themselves at trying to restrain the tides of their affections. They say to themselves, I love so intensely, I must love less; and they attempt to do it; and they cannot, any more than the tides can help flowing in. And so they are full of trouble, because they think they may be failing somehow in fealty to God. Now, be sure of this: the more you love those whom God has given you, the more rightly religious are you; the more are you doing as God would have you; the more are you standing in the blessed sunshine of his smile. Nobody ever loved wife, husband, child, brother, sister, too much. The *intensity* of your affection is not wrong. Love until your love floats and carries off your nature in its sacred freshet. That is righteous, that is religious, that is as God would have it. Thus, you are not idolatrous. It is only when your affection *interferes with truth and duty* that you have sunk your love into idolizing. Here was Rebecca's wrong. Jacob was more to her than truth, than God. Jacob was so much to her that, for his sake, she would lend herself to evil. So she was idolatrous. Intensity of affection is not idolizing. Interference, for affection's sake, with the highest right, that is idolizing.

And so idolatrous Rebecca sets herself at work to teach her best loved Jacob fraud. Oh, to what pitiable purposes even our affections may be perverted! To what loose ends we fall when we forget the right! What a tangle, thus, does our life become! Why, this woman is all unsexed. It is Lady Macbeth in Scripture. Nothing thinks *she* of the good Duncan. Nothing thinks Rebecca of the dim-eyed Isaac, of the defrauded Esau, of the righteous character, even, of the Jacob whom she loves. She will twist him even full of deceits. She will bid him even run the risk of the cursing which wrong brings. How cruel wrong is always! If right is safest, it is always kindliest too.

This is idolizing, when, like Rebecca, we let our love draw us from the truth for love's sake.

CONCERNING SIN.

TAKE, for example, that sin of Jacob's in his seizure of the blessing.

Consider, like all sins, it was a sin first in thought. Some plotting purpose to get the better of his brother Esau had long dwelt in Jacob's mind. Such thought was in him years back, when he wrenched the promise of the birthright from him. It is the powder of bad thoughts which the tinder of occasion sets aflash. As a man "thinketh in his heart, so is he." Here is always the guilt in germ,—in the admitted thought. All temptations and all occasions to sin are powerless, except so far as they fall in with previous meditations upon the guilt. Be more anxious that you think rightly than that you do rightly. Pure thinking will make pure doing. We are safe only as we bring our thought into captivity to Christ.

Consider, it was a sin, like all sins, urging on

into deeper and wider sinning. He will first prepare to do the lie—he puts on the skins, and takes the meat he means to have his father think is venison. Next, he will speak the lie, "I am Esau, thy first-born." Next, he will build the fortification of profanity about the lie,—he will use, impiously, the eternal name: "The Lord thy God brought it me." And so beginning, he is pushed on into all manner of deceptions. Everything about him is a lie.

"Happy the man," says Robertson, "who cannot, even from the faint shadows of his own experience, comprehend the desperate agony of such a state; the horror mixed with hardening effrontery with which a man feels himself compelled to take step after step, and is aware at last that he is drifting, drifting from the great shore of Truth, like one carried out by the tide against his will, till he finds himself at last in a sea of falsehood; his whole life one great ocean of false appearance." Sinning is like sliding upon those great ice-hills they have in Canada, in the winter. You cannot just tip your sled or bit of ice over the top, and slide a foot or two and then stop,—start and you go.

Consider, here was a sin to which Jacob was tempted even by his own mother, and yet that did not excuse. Oh, this tremendous solitariness of sin appalls me often! I may find palliations, but I never can find such excuses as shall lift the responsibility from my separate soul when I have done a wrong. That is the trouble, that I have done it.

Consider, this was a sin along which the divine purpose flowed to its accomplishment; thus the prophecy came to its fulfillment, that the elder should serve the younger; but this did not make it less a sin. Out of the hard-headed and hard-hearted bigotry and cruelty of Philip the Second of Spain, God brought religious liberty to Europe and America, through the gates of the Dutch Republic. But, because God did thus, Philip the Second was no less, perhaps, the most infernal king who ever sat upon a throne. When God makes even the wrath of man to praise him, that does not change man's wrath to righteousness. Great truth—sin cannot disappoint or hinder God; but in this shining truth I can find no license for sinning.

Consider, this sin was a *seed* which Jacob planted. That is the constant trouble with men. They think that sinning is sowing stones instead of seeds. Put a stone into the ground, and that is the end of it. It will lie there. It will come to nothing. You have planted a bit of rock, and that is all. Put a seed into the ground, and you have started something on the way toward fruitage, and toward such fruitage as is wrapped up in the brown capsule. That is the trouble with sinning. It is seed planting, not pebble planting. It is not that you have done a wrong, and will now have done with it. You cannot have done with it. You have started something toward fruitage, toward the sort of fruitage which belongs to the evil deed which you have done. "Whatsoever a man soweth *that* shall he also reap." Nothing is more striking in the whole Scripture than the sight of Jacob reaping himself, through his whole life, that which he had sown. Notice, he gets the birthright and the blessing through his mean fraud; but, somehow or other, the deed turns on him, and he gets what he so stooped to gain, defrauded of everything which makes it valuable. He is first and chief, but he is first and chief in exile. Among his kinsmen, in the enjoyment of the honors and emoluments of that which he has gained, he may not stay. Esau will slay him. Rebecca is alarmed; she must save the son she loves so much; out of her sight he must go. Not as the inheritor of the promises ought to go, as a prince, and with a princely retinue; but on a desolate, difficult, dangerous journey, through wastes of sand, and in perils of banditti, he must go, a lonely pilgrim, a fugitive exile, through four hundred and fifty menacing miles, before he can be assured of safety among his mother's relatives in Haran. This thing which he has won is a poor stripped thing, after all.

Ah, we reap harvests like the seeds we sow! "Do men gather grapes of thorns or figs of thistles?"

DIVINE REMEDY FOR SIN.

NOT long since an engineer was running a passenger express train through from Philadelphia to Jersey City. It was one of the swiftest trains, and heaviest, such as are intrusted only to the most experienced engineers. As the train was going, a heavy connecting-rod of the driving-wheel on the right of the engine broke, and one end of it, swinging upwards, struck the cab beneath the engineer and shattered it to a thousand pieces. The man fell senseless on the engine. He was both burned and scalded. The pain quickly restored consciousness. The engine, with its train, was rushing forward with fearful velocity to certain destruction. Inside the long train of cars, men were reading, sleeping, talking, laughing. Inside the long train of cars, women were playing with their babies. The fireman jumped from the tender and managed to escape. The engineer might have escaped as well, but he crept along the side of the engine, and with his burned hands got hold of the lever, reversed the engine, and applied the air-brakes. Now, do you not see that the engineer was the real saviour of that train? that he took upon himself all the terrible death which menaced that whole train, and daring it himself, thrust its greedy, awful shadow back from these men and mothers and little children?

Or take this other more historic story, how, one night, after a great battle, when his men were utterly exhausted, the great Napoleon was pacing about the camp, and came upon a tired sentinel asleep. Then the emperor took upon himself the obedience of the soldier, and paced his beat for him until he awoke, and then gave him back his musket. Can you not see how Napoleon took the place of that sentinel, doing his duty, and suffering the pain of sleeplessness in his stead, and so kept back from him the penalty for sleeping at his post?

Of course, such instances as these are but the dimmest possible figures of the immense truths wrapped up in the atonement; but they are at least dim figures. I cannot find the doctrine of a substitutionary atonement out of relation and awry with the facts of life. I do not find it difficult of belief. To me, it seems to mate itself with every noble deed of self-sacrifice; with everything most worthy and most praiseful in the best human moods; with every parental pain and service for the child's sake; and tying itself into beautiful analogy with all these, to be itself the utmost and consummate flower of them all.

Listen to these words from Professor Henry, late of the Smithsonian Institution. They are among the last he ever wrote. He was no dreaming sentimentalist, he was no loose thinker; he was a keen-eyed man of science, he was an adept in searching facts and estimating them. He would not have been at the head of the Smithsonian Institution at Washington, had he not been. These were what he considers the facts of the human life and conscience: "In my own mind I find ideas of right and wrong, of good and evil. These ideas then exist in the universe, and therefore form a basis of our ideas of the moral universe. Furthermore, the conceptions of good which are found among our ideas associated with evil can be attributed only to a being of infinite perfection like that which we denominate God. On the other hand, *we are conscious of having such evil thoughts and tendencies that we cannot associate ourselves with a Divine Being who is the Director and Governor of all, or even call upon him for mercy, without the intercession of one who may affiliate himself with us.*"

These, then, are the ideas which Professor Henry declares to be scientific. God holy; man sinful; chasm between the holy God and the sinful man; that chasm to be bridged only by an intercessor affiliating God with us. Where can you see such intercessor bringing God and man together, standing for man and yet satisfying God? Only at the cross can you see him— man himself, and taking upon himself man's duty and doing it, and taking upon himself man's death and dying it, and so honoring the law and expiating sin; and yet also God himself—bringing God and man together. Here, then, may I see the divine remedy for sin in the blood of the Divine Victim, who was human, and therefore in him humanity met the doom of guilt; who was divine, and who therefore could sustain and exhaust the doom.

Captain Hedley Vickers, smitten under a sense of sin, came to his table one morning broken-hearted and crying out, "Oh, wretched man that I am!" As he said the words he chanced to glance at his Bible, which lay open before him. Suddenly his eyes rested on that Scripture: "The blood of Jesus Christ, his Son, cleanseth us from all sin." "Then," said he, "it can cleanse me from mine;" and instantly believing, he was filled with joy and peace. From that hour to the time when he fell in the trenches before Sebastapol, he was in peace. Ah, Hedley Vickers, you could get peace nowhere else, because you could see remedy for sin nowhere else save in the blood of the cross!

CHRIST THE LIGHT.

CHRIST is the light for life which guides. "I am the light of the world," he says. What the fire-pillar was to the Israelites, marking out their way as they toiled through some difficult night-march, that is Christ to men to-day. Our Lord said these words during the feast of tabernacles, when two huge candelabra, burning in the temple courts, shot out their radiance; and, just as no court in Jerusalem, no leafy booth out on the hill-side, but might get radiance and guidance from those huge temple lights, streaming their rays out into the darkness, so there is no man who may not receive the illumination shining forth from Christ. He did not say he was the Light for any special persons, or races, or nations. "I am the Light of the *world*," he said.

Nothing is truer than that men need this light for guidance. I have been reading a wonderfully interesting book, called "The Conflict of Christianity with Heathenism," by Dr. Ullhorn. It is the story of the grandest fight that was ever waged, and the most marvelous victory that was ever won—that of a little believing company, who rejoiced in the light of Christ, and took him for guidance, with and over the hoary heathenism and mighty systems of philosophy which did not know and would not see the light of Christ. This need of even the greatest men—in war, in government, in thought—for some sure and shining guidance, comes out constantly and most pathetically in these pages. This is what Pliny used to say: "There is nothing certain save that everything is uncertain, and there is no more wretched and yet arrogant being than man. The best thing that has been given to man, amid the many trials of this life, is that he can take his own life." Julius Cæsar could conquer Gaul and found an empire; he could and did say, that he did not believe in the diverse and warring gods of heathenism; but, notwithstanding, he was all the time held in such terrible and superstitious fear of something, he could tell scarcely what, that he never thought of stepping into a chariot without first muttering some magical formula as a preservative against accident. The great Augustus, who was so great that he could take up and carry on and so substantiate the work of Cæsar, that the Roman Empire should stand thenceforward for more than a thousand years, and who sometimes scoffed openly at the gods of heathenism, was, nevertheless, so bound and blinded by superstitious fear, that he would dread misfortune through the entire day if, on rising in the morning, he had chanced to put the left sandal on the right foot.

That heathen culture, lifted as it was, was always cruel. It could gladly glut itself at the sight of blood in the arena, when, for its holiday amusement, gladiators and captives fought to the death. It could make sport at the misfortune of others; it used to have idiots about itself, not that it might love them, but that it might laugh at them. The wife of Seneca had such an idiot for her sport. The poor thing grew blind before her death; and, the wonder of it was, did not know that she was blind, but thought the house dark—that was all. Seneca was a great man; so great that he could write things that sounded so much like precepts of the New Testament that some have thought he must have had intercourse with the apostle Paul, though there is no evidence of that; but he confesses that he could not find the light. Of this poor fool Hapaste, at whom they used to laugh in the house of Seneca, because she did not know she was blind, he writes: "But you may be sure that this at which we laugh in her happens to us all. The blind seek for a guide; we wander about without a guide."

Now Christ says to all the world, "I am the Guide for life; I am the world's Light."

He is such a guiding Light because he *is* the Light. Moral guidance shines from him, because he is the one perfect specimen of moral living. Constantine the Great was the worshiper of Apollo, and Apollo was the god of the sun. His army numbered but forty thousand men. The army of Maxentius, his adversary, numbered three times that. Constantine was in great doubt and trouble. What should he do? Whither should he turn? He knew the God of the Christians. But should he worship Apollo, or their God? Then he saw, one day, a wondrous sign. The sun was declining in the west, but upon the sun, and brighter than the sun, he saw a cross, and around it, in gleaming letters, "By this sign conquer." Thenceforward the cross shone on his banners, and by this sign he did conquer.

We may call it legend, but the truth for us within the legend is, that as that cross outshone the sun, so the light of Christ's example outshines all other radiance. He is the Light for guidance, because he *is* the Light. As the sun paled behind that cross, so every other guide for life pales and dims in comparison with him. I get from him the light of perfect moral guidance, because he is the perfect man.

TRUE SELF-INTEREST.

HERE is the key-board of a musical instrument. Some of the notes are higher and some are lower, yet all are equally legitimate musical notes, and all are necessary to the sounding of the entire harmony.

Here is the key-board of motives by which a human soul is played upon—I mean that key-board which God uses, not that the devil uses. Some motives you can call lower and some higher, yet all are motives rightful, and all are motives needful, that the soul may send back answering melody to God.

When the Lord says, "Seek ye first the kingdom of God and his righteousness, and all these things shall be added unto you," he plays upon the motive of an enlightened self-interest. To translate it into our common speech, the Lord says that supreme choice of God and steady service of his righteousness pay better than any other sort of life, since, in the long run, to that choice and service these other and lower worldly boons are surest to gather. Supreme choice of God and a steady service of his righteousness are a better investment than the overtopping choice of self and the service of wrong. So, too, in this other Scripture, God touches with his finger the same key of motive. "For what is a man advantaged if he gain the whole world and lose himself, or be cast away?" To choose wrong and to get at last the wreck of wrong, though in that choice you become for the time the possessor of the whole world, is a bad bargain—is, everything considered, the worst thing you can do for yourself. The motive touched upon is that of a true self-interest, call it a lower motive, if you please. that Francis Xavier sung:

> My God, I love thee; not because
> I hope for heaven thereby,
> Nor yet because who love thee not
> Must burn eternally.

Thou, O my Jesus, thou didst me
    Upon the cross embrace;
For me didst bear the nails, and spear,
    And manifold disgrace,

And griefs and torments numberless,
    And sweat of agony,
Yea, death itself, and all for me
    Who was thine enemy.

Then why, O blessed Jesus Christ,
    Should I not love thee still?
Not for the hope of winning heaven,
    Nor of escaping hell;

Not with the hope of gaining aught,
    Not seeking a reward;
But as thyself hast loved me,
    O ever-loving Lord.

So would I love thee, dearest Lord,
    And in thy praise will sing;
Solely because thou art my God,
    And my eternal king.

And that, you say, is the highest, noblest, most celestial motive—the motive of a true love, which thinks only of its object and nothing of the reward this object can bestow. And what you say is true.

But it is also true that other motives must be

struck, in order that this higher one may be. Before you can get the bloom you must have the seed, and the seed buried under ground. Because the bloom is better than the seed, you do not therefore despise the seed.

An enlightened self-interest is not selfishness —though it is often crudely and carelessly confounded with it. If God should say to you, "Be sure you enter heaven, because there is only just so much heaven, and if you do not get it, somebody else will; seize your chance, therefore, and get in first, and so crowd others out"—that would be an appeal to selfishness, for selfishness is love of self beyond others; is the determination to get the best for self at the cost of others. But a true and enlightened self-interest is a desire to be the best and to get the best that one can and one ought, not at the cost of others, but without injury to others.

To selfishness God never appeals, because the motive is a wrong one.

To a true self-interest, to a desire to be and to have that which is really worth the having and the being, God does appeal; for that motive is a right one.

Certainly nothing can be truer, and nothing can be more right, than that I, a soul weighted with an eternal destiny, should desire, and determine to reach, the most shining destiny possible for myself.

It is not a question as towards others. Nobody will have less of heaven, because by God's good grace at last I enter it. It is a question for myself. It is a question demanding answer from a true self-interest, and this desire for the best good of the self, that the soul may rise into the glorious realm and possession God means the soul should rise to, is a desire rightful and legitimate, and one which God does appeal to when he beseeches me not to make a bad bargain for myself, and though I may win the world, yet lose myself.

CONQUERING PROMISE.

STALWART and girdling promise this—" So shall my word be that goeth forth out of my mouth; it shall not return unto me void, but it shall accomplish that which I please, and it shall prosper in the thing whereto I sent it."

That is to say, there has been some definite, divine word spoken about the world. That word is sure to be filled with fact. It shall be brimmed with the accomplishment of the divine pleasure. It shall go, as an arrow to its target, straight to the mark of the divine purpose.

Like the snow and rain, shall this word be, the prophet has been saying. Not heedlessly do the rains fall. Not uselessly do the snows cast their white mantles upon the hills. Through them the sower wins his seed, and the eater bread. So shall God's word be. It has a meaning and a ministry. Not so sure is the harvest, as its fulfillment. Not so certain is the budding of the spring after the snows have done their duty, as is the glad accomplishment of God's word about the world. It shall not return unto him void. It shall prosper in the thing whereto he has sent it.

Constantly do men join issue with the prophet here. In many quarters it is just now fashionable to do it. "What you say, O prophet, is a poor and pitiable dream," they say. "This idea of a divine word about the world, and of a divine purpose accomplishing itself in the world, is a figment, a chimera."

"There is no God," says a certain sort of science; exclaiming with Lalande, "for sixty years I have surveyed the heavens, and never as yet have I seen him." And again writes Laplace, "In my heaven I can find no God." Of course, therefore, this non-existent being can have no thought or word about the world.

"First and foremost we must strike at the idea of God," says Socialism, arranging its combinations, and burning its Paris, and seizing the railroads with its riots. "The thought of God we must wrench out of people's minds. He is nothing but the bug-a-boo, with which to frighten children. We neither wish to know, or care for what may be, his thought about the world."

And the prevailing skepticism of the time has bitten with its chill many hearts which would not dare or wish to call themselves unchristian. Like the virgins in the parable, their lamps of faith and hope are going out, and they wonder whether, after all, the God in whom their fathers trusted has spoken any mighty and triumphant word, or is pushing on any overcoming purpose about the world.

But, though you may sleep all day, the sun still shines. Though to you the mountain may be draped in mists, it has not unloosened its granite roots. Though you may be caught amid the swirling snows, the spring is hastening on. Though you may deny, or though you may doubt, God's word about the world has been spoken, and every passing year is hurrying to add its syllable to its magnificent significance.

Glance at a single illustration. I open Merivale's "History of the Romans Under the Empire." I read that the first and great Emperor Augustus, toward the close of his reign, drew up with his own hand a complete survey of the vast dominion over which he swayed the sceptre. This *Breviarium*, as he called it, he placed in the hands of the Vestal Virgins, to be delivered to the Senate and his successor after his death. It was a succinct but authentic statement of all the resources of the Roman people. It detailed the state of the naval and military forces; the number of the citizens, and subjects, and allies; the condition of the provinces and dependencies; the political system of each one of the various communities which went to make up the empire; the amount of the public revenues; the proceeds of every import; the expenses of the general government.

When I read of such a consummate governmental compendium, I am anxious to know where the great emperor found the accurate information upon which to base it all.

I find that at three several times during his great reign he ordered a complete census and taxing of his vast empire. Reading of this *Breviarium*, I see the reason for his careful census. He wished to organize his empire. He wished to know what the sceptre he wielded meant. He wished to find out the directest and most controlling way of government. He wished to discover what, in the way of revenue, he could depend on. He was emperor. He was statesman. Such was his statesman-like thought and purpose.

All this is very interesting and important. It is a most luminous and noteworthy fact of history.

But a new and very tremendous significance is given to this wise purpose of the great emperor when I find that, though Augustus on the world's topmost throne was all unconscious of it, God used it and overruled it for the greatest accomplishment of his word about the world.

What knew the lifted emperor, or what cared he about a peasant baby who was born on some night in a cattle's cavern, in the little Jewish town of Bethlehem? It was not a very surprising thing that a baby should be born; and Bethlehem was one of the smallest hamlets in one of the obscurest corners of that world-including empire. But this child was God manifest in the flesh. And it was God's word about this child, that he should first see the light in Bethlehem—in no other spot. But she who was to be the mother of the child was dwelling then in Nazareth in Galilee, a town separated from Bethlehem by a difficult and distant journey. But she was forced to Bethlehem at just the birth-time of the child. What forced her there? One of the orders of census-taking and of taxing of this emperor.

He was one of the lesser prophets. He was one who did not fill a very large place either in eminence or in service. But this was the word of God, through this prophet, about the divine child, said seven hundred years before the birth-time: "But thou, Bethlehem Ephratah, though thou be little among the thousands of Judah, yet out of thee shall he come forth unto me that is to be ruler in Israel; whose goings forth have been from of old, from everlasting."

And the Roman Emperor, the greatest and most exalted man of his age, thinking only about discovering the resources of his empire, thinking only about gathering data for his *Breviarium,* is the unconscious and freely acting, yet still compelled agent to pour into that word of God the most perfect significance of fulfillment. The Roman Emperor is the subject of the word of God. The Roman Emperor is the tributary to Jesus Christ.

Now, in the light of this conquering promise, it is certainly right and fair for me to generalize to other promises, and to be sure that they are just as conquering. The world is not at loose ends. God leads. God has spoken. No least word of his shall fail or fall. Here is courage for me. If I work with God, I cannot meet defeat; I must be on the winning side of things.

PRAYERS DENIED YET ANSWERED.

GOD is not distant from the world. God has not flung the world from his creative hand, to let it get on as best it may. The chasm between this world and the throne of God is not so wide that he who fills immensity with his presence cannot be both on that throne and in the world. The creative hand of God is now his providential hand. The life of the world is life to which God lends energy. The breath of the new spring is the breath of God. The petal of a lily is a canvas for his color. The sweep of a sparrow's wing and the moment of a sparrow's fall are not matters too slight for his notice and appointment. As James Martineau has spoken of it: "God is excluded from neither air, nor earth, nor sea, nor souls. There is a mystic implication of his nature with ours, and ours with his; his serenity amid our griefs; his sanctity amid our guilt; his wakefulness amid our sleep; his life through our death; his silence amid our stormy force." "Thou hast beset me behind and before and laid thine hand upon me," exclaims the Psalmist.

If, then, God be in such neighborhood with us, prayer cannot be irrational. He is within whisper reach, within thought reach. Nay, if we will accept the Bible statement, we must believe that the divine attention is alert to catch the voice of prayer. God waits for it, searches for it, solicits it. The Father seeketh for the worship of those who worship him in spirit and in truth. The prayer of the upright is his delight, and also prayer is answered. The Psalms are full of the pæans of this praise: "I cried unto the Lord with my voice, and he heard me out of his holy hill." "Blessed be the Lord, because he hath heard the voice of my supplications." Christ asks: "Do you think you are more tender in your fatherhood than the Heavenly Father is in his; or what man is there of you who, if his son ask bread, will he give him a stone, or, if he ask a fish, will he give him a serpent? If ye, then, being evil, know how to give good gifts to your children, how much more shall your Father which is in heaven give good things to them that ask him."

But while it is true that the besetting God delights in prayer, and that often the answer comes swift as the stroke of the wing of Gabriel, or suddenly as the knock of a disimprisoned Peter upon the door of the house of Mary, it is also just as true that sometimes there is a black and wide and weary chasm between the prayer and the answer of it. The prayer goes up, but the pain goes on. The cry goes forth, but the burden galls and crushes down. The ear of God seems heavy and his hands idle, while the heart, sick with hope deferred, and weary with its groanings, seems to stand on an iron earth, and to stretch the hands of a useless supplication toward a brazen heaven.

Take a Scriptural illustration. There was a family in Bethany which Jesus loved. Many a time, from the conflicts with the Scribes and

Pharisees, from the weariness of his pilgrimage, from the hardness of his poverty, like a vessel, storm-beaten, putting into a quiet harbor, he had sought grateful refuge here. It is only lately that he has been a most welcome guest. He has gone now into Perea, beyond the Jordan. During his absence, Lazarus, the brother, and support of the household, sickens. The disease runs rapidly to a crisis; death is evidently in dangerous neighborhood. Naturally enough, the sisters turn in their extremity to the Lord they love. A messenger is hurriedly dispatched to Jesus. He bears from the sisters as true and trustful and beautiful a prayer as was ever offered. It is full of a most touching confidence. "Lord, he whom thou lovest is sick." It is but a day's journey from Bethabara to Bethany. Certainly, there will be no tarrying. Certainly, their Lord will not wait now, when the sincerest faith frames his own love into gentle argument for haste.

But he does tarry, even though the sisters watch there for him; even though Lazarus, whom he loves, is sick. The prayer goes up to the Lord of power and of life; but it comes back with empty hands. The sisters attend their brother, but they are helpless. Here is Lazarus dying, and there is Jesus waiting over in Bethabara. Death comes on quick and conquering. "Now, when he had heard that Lazarus was sick, he abode two days still in the same place where he was." The very need at Bethany seems to be a reason for his leisure at Bethabara; and when at last he does come, slowly moving on—consuming twice the time needful for the journey—as far as Lazarus is concerned, he might have stayed at Bethabara. When he reaches Bethany, Lazarus has been four days buried; and, in that hot Eastern climate, corruption has long ago set in.

Well, does not this action of our Lord bring into view another fact concerning prayer—that sometimes it seems to be a void and useless thing? The Lord waits; he does not hasten. You dispatch your prayer; but, meanwhile, Lazarus dies, and must be buried. Your trouble greatens; your distress gets more distressful; your pain pierces with sharper pangs; your thorn in the flesh grows larger and cuts deeper; and, though you wait and watch for answer, like those who watch for the morning, all that is left you is just to watch and wait, saying over, as again and again Martha and Mary murmured each to each: "Oh! if our Lord had been here, our brother had not died." But your Lord is not there. He lingers at Bethabara, and all you can do is to moan in helpless anguish, in the cruel companionship of your distress.

It is a very real experience in life, Mary and Martha bemoaning their dead brother in Bethany and Jesus abiding in Bethabara. It is John Bunyan's "Valley of the Shadow of Death," where the paths are steep, and the rocks are hard, and the sky is black, and the spaces are thronged with tormenting shapes of doubt, and God seems nowhere.

The question arises, "What is the *Divine Reason* behind such experience?" If God has no benignant reason, he is cruel. Possibly we may discover such. Let us look into the chapter which holds the story, and attempt it.

Here is one reason. Our Lord sometimes waits in Bethabara, when we need him in Bethany, *that he may furnish us with larger reason for faith in him.* This was the explanation of our Lord's absence from the dying-bed of Lazarus. He said to his disciples: "I am glad for your sakes that I was not there, to the intent ye might believe." No life can get on without faith. Columbus waited eighteen years for three small vessels, not as large or as strong as your common coasting schooners, with which to search out America; but he believed that somewhere amid the western waters there was an undiscovered continent; and that faith sustained him, and by it he conquered. It is impossible that life accomplish anything in any direction, except it be able to fling the grappling anchor flukes of its faith into somewhat worthy. Every one of the Bible-roll of heroes, in the eleventh chapter of Hebrews, had been a nerveless and defeated man had he not had faith. "This man will do somewhat," said one of a great Reformer, "because he believes somewhat." But there can be no faith, except there be an underlying reason. Reason must be the pedestal upon which faith stands, that it may gain wider vision and discern substantial shapes in the shadowy future. Faith without reason is fanaticism—blind, unreasonable, dogged impulse. Columbus had reason for his faith, that somewhere a western continent balanced the eastern, because of the globular shape of the earth, just then proven, and because of other geographical and scientific facts. Now, a religious life is one impelled and inspired by a faith in a personal, loving, guarding God. The soul is weak and perplexed, and dim of eye, and feeble of foot and arm; but the soul—looking out from itself toward God by faith, discerns his strength, his clear knowledge, the promise of his uplifting, lives not in itself, but in its God; takes to itself the power and light and love of God; and, like a child, sure that it is safe and supplied because it is folded in the mother's arms, rejoices in a rapturous security, because it is gathered into the Infinite Bosom. But is it not true that God must somehow show himself to be a God like this, before your faith or mind can fasten on him?

Precisely such ground for faith did not our Lord yield his disciples and these sisters through his tarrying at Bethabara? Lazarus was dead. He had been four days lying in that tomb. Death had begun to wanton on him. The sisters had sent forth their prayer; but he had tarried. But in our Lord's triumph over the dark death of Lazarus, through the power of his resurrection, did he not disclose to these, and, through them, to us, indestructible reason for victorious faith? "To the intent ye might believe." Sometimes our Lord tarries, not that we may in the end believe him less, but that we may believe him more.

Then, too, sometimes our Lord tarries at Bethabara, when we need him at Bethany, *because thus he is enabled to do better for us than we have asked*. God is no niggardly giver. He does not stint the fullness of his answer to the pitiable measure of our poor prayer. He would do for us exceedingly abundantly above all that we can ask or think. How much larger the answer to the prayer of these sisters than the measure of the prayer itself! They asked but that he should heal Lazarus. He would give them, not simply Lazarus healed from sickness, but Lazarus made a conqueror over the great conqueror. He would flood their souls with the streams of consolation of which that mighty miracle was the fountain. What were death now to Martha and to Mary, and to the disciples, if death were but a thrall beneath the absolute sway of their loving Lord? But these stricken ones at Bethany entered into this magnificence of divine response through their Lord's delay.

But, also, our Lord sometimes stays in Bethabara, when we need him in Bethany, *because we can do more to glorify him, if he delay, than if he should come.* "This sickness is for the glory of God, that the Son of God might be glorified thereby." Lazarus, through his weakness and death, did more for Jesus than he could have done had he preached the gospel in all the world. Charlotte Elliot, imprisoned in her sick chamber, but singing, "Just as I am, without one plea," did more for her Lord's gospel than she could have accomplished, possibly, had he dis-imprisoned her. Looking back upon it now, from the heavenly heights, John Bunyan must see that those twelve years in Bedford Jail, in which imprisonment yielded him leisure to dream and write of the journey from the City of Destruction, were more fruitful for the triumph of his Lord's truth than any years of free and active preaching could have been. To glorify him, is the Christian aim. Sometimes Bethabara keeps our Lord from our Bethany, because, through his absence, his glory can more shiningly disclose itself.

So here the prayer which seemed denied was yet answered in the best and largest way. Let not waiting hearts at Bethany fail then utterly, if the Lord do tarry at Bethabara.

"All things work together for good." Wonderful Scripture! And yet how plainly may it be seen in this narrative! The sickening, dying brother; the helpless sisters; the tomb; the corruption even—all wrought for the good of a firmer basis for faith; of a larger answer than they had ever dreamed; of the sunrise of his power upon the night of human death.

RESOURCE IN TROUBLE.

LET us take note of and profit by the example of the early Christians in their trouble. Peter had healed the lame man at the gate called Beautiful. The miracle and his preaching had stirred the multitude afresh. Many had believed. The Sanhedrim had arraigned the apostle and his companion John. They had commanded them not to speak at all, nor teach henceforward in the name of Jesus. "We cannot but speak the things which we have seen and heard," had been their answer; and then, let go, they had gone to their own company.

It was no slight thing to brave the anger of the Jewish leaders. It meant, to those who dared to do it, oppression, imprisonment, probable death. But these early Christians had a resource in the danger and trouble gathering around them. Let us think a moment of their resource.

"And when they had heard what Peter and John had said, they lifted up their voice to God with one accord, and said: Lord, thou art God, which hast made heaven and earth, and the sea, and all that in them is."

Their resource was in a *God Almighty*, the Maker of heaven and earth and sea. It is good sometimes to think of the affluence of the Divine Power. The sun is the central object in our heavens. His diameter is eleven hundred and twelve times that of our own earth. His surface is twelve thousand, six hundred and eleven times that of our own earth. His light is twenty-two thousand million times that of the most brilliant star. That sun is the source of the light and heat by means of which all the processes of life are carried on in this earth of ours. And yet the two thousand three hundred millionth part of the force radiated by the sun is all our earth can grasp of his lighting and heating rays streaming out in all directions. It is but by this pitiable fraction of the sun's mighty power that all the earth's work is done. The Scripture figure of our God is that he is a Sun. We have a right to press the figure. So *superabounding* is his power, that the smallest fraction of it is enough for our utmost need.

These early Christians had a resource in *an all-wise God*. A thousand years before, David, in the second Psalm, had prophesied this very trouble. This troubling storm against thy Christ and Truth neither surprises nor disappoints thee. Thou sawest what must be, and this trouble too thou sawest. Disastrous as it seems to us, it is shining clear to thee. Thou art all-wise.

These early Christians found a resource in *an all-controlling God*. "For to do whatsoever thy hand and thy counsel determined before to be done." Mystery here certainly. That old problem of the divine control and of the freeness of the human will emerges. We may not attempt to clear the thick mists away. We cannot do it. But we may anchor to the great helpful truth. God controls. Everything moves along the line of his great purpose. Not the wildest rage of men can slip that predetermined track.

These early Christians found a resource in this almighty, all-wise, all-controlling God, *laid hold of by their prayer.* "And when they heard that, they lifted up their voices to God with one accord." There was no thought with them that such a God could not and would not answer. No breath so prevailing and so real to them as praying breath.

These early Christians found a resource, too, in *self-surrender.* They asked, not so much to be delivered from the storm, as that they might carry themselves worthily while it raged. They asked, not so much for sunnier skies and smoother paths, as that they might be saved from faltering, though the clouds might crowd and the rocks cut their persistent feet. It was the noblest of prayers they uttered: that they might give themselves to God's will, and get that carried on at any hazard. "Grant unto thy servants that with all boldness they may speak thy word." It was as though they had said: "Lord, we accept the trouble; it is not about this blustering Jewish tempest we are so much concerned; but we are anxious that it should not blow away our faith and courage. Save us, O Lord, from that."

This, then, was the resource of these early Christians in their trouble: self-surrender to the will of the prayer-moved, all-controlling, all-wise, almighty God. This *is* resource; for it is an utter and intelligent *taking sides with God*. It is transmuting trouble into blessed grace. It is refusing to be scared from God by trouble; it is rather determining that trouble shall shut us but the closer up to God.

Let us use the resource. It is one thing, and it is a too frequent thing, to let trouble make a chasm between ourselves and God. That is to bring upon ourselves a terrible helplessness. It is another thing to so manage our trouble that it shall force us to take sides with God in it; and then trouble is baffled, and we are kept; for we are embosomed in the Infinite."

ALL THINGS WORKING TOGETHER FOR GOOD.

PLINY, the Roman philosopher, had a friend Correlius, to whom he was devotedly attached. The death of this friend was to Pliny the bitterest bereavement. He searched everywhere for comfort, but could find it neither in his philosophy, nor amid the thronging gods of his religion. His appeal for comfort, in a letter which he writes to another friend, is one of the most touching passages in ancient literature. "Speak comfort to me. Tell me not that Correlius was old and infirm, and that his death was by natural law. All this I know. But supply me with some reflections that are uncommon and resistless; that neither the wisdom of the world, nor the precepts of the philosophers can teach me. For all that I have heard and all that I have read occur to me of themselves; but all these are by far too weak to support me under such affliction."

The question is, is there anywhere such uncommon and resistless comfort as that which Pliny so passionately calls for? Has any such ever come from anywhere to smitten men and women? Is there any underlying and comprehensive and pervasive truth, which can bleach, at least to some extent, the black and frowning face of sorrow; which can take, in anywise, the pang out of the pain? Suppose that Pliny had written to the Apostle Paul instead of his friend, Calestrius Tiro, asking comfort—could Paul have given it to him? Certainly Paul could. This he would have said to him, for he did say it to other people of Pliny's time, just as tried and buffeted as Pliny was: "Give yourself to God; choose him supremely; love him, and then be sure of this—all things work together for good to them that love God." All things—that is as comprehensive as possible; that includes bereavements, disasters, pains, troubles, diseases, crampings of poverty, anything, everything. We are to know that anything and everything works together for good to them that love God. Here certainly is constant and ever-coming comfort.

It is at the point of faith that the main difficulty lies. If, but with a faith as sure as that with which we seize the fact that the sun will rise to-morrow morning, we could seize this fact, we should then be settled and stilled in a comfort, the steady and joyful heart of which no arm of disaster, how bony and long soever, could reach possibly. We should be, as to our inner hearts, hung and swung as are compasses on shipboard; so that in whatever way the storm may pitch and toss the vessel, the compass maintains its level.

For the help of our faith, in this strong consolation, let us take an instance from the life of Paul himself. It was with Paul a persistent prayer and purpose that he might preach the Lord Jesus in the capital city of the world. Cities then, as now, were the fountains of power. Paul was the apostle to the Gentiles, and Rome was the heart and spring of Gentile influence. A church had been gathered there, which needed apostolic training. For many reasons to Paul, the divine call seemed to be sounding toward Rome.

But between Paul and Rome there were lifted the hostile hands of many obstacles. It was a long and difficult journey from Corinth, round by Jerusalem, to Rome. It was an expensive journey. Dangers of all sorts thronged it. Toward Paul, there was peculiar danger from Jewish hatred. When he announced his intention of going to Jerusalem, and from thence to Rome, it was at this point of Jewish hostility that the implorations of his Christian brethren made loving assault. Besides, the Holy Ghost witnessed that in every city bonds and imprisonments awaited him. Then, too, having reached Rome, obstacles would not cease. There Jewish cunning would seek to circumvent him, and Jewish spite destroy him, except he could be somehow under the special protection of the government. But how could he, hated and slandered as he was, gain such protection?

Paul starts upon his journey; and, on the way,

at first sight, there seem to be nothing but hindrances and disasters for him. There is the mob at Jerusalem. There is the trial before Felix at Cæsarea, which comes to nothing. There are the two weary years of imprisonment at that city. There is, at last, the appeal to Cæsar. Then there are the voyage and the shipwreck and the delay. And when, after years of waiting, Paul finds himself passing the gates of Rome, he enters them a prisoner.

But look at these seeming hindrances and disasters in their deeper and real relation to the furtherance of the apostolic purpose. The two years' imprisonment issues in the appeal to Cæsar. That appeal makes him a sacred person in the eye of the Roman law. No Jew can touch him. No mob can seize him with violent hand. The journey is long and expensive; but forced to appeal to Cæsar, he takes the journey to the throne of the Emperor at the expense of the Roman government. The shipwreck is baffling, but his courage and calm self-poise win the defending admiration of Julius, the Centurion; so that when he reaches Rome, Julius makes special exertion in his behalf, and gains for him the privilege, not enjoyed without a special order, to live in his own hired lodging, and to freely see his friends. In Rome, his trial is delayed two years, and during all this time the strong arm of the government shields him from both Jew and Gentile. His imprisonment gives him the constant, yet changing audience of the one soldier who guards him; thus the saints begin to multiply in Cæsar's household. So, too, as he writes to the Philippians, his very bonds help on the preaching of his Lord. Also, his imprisonment gives him leisure to write the great Epistles to the Ephesians, to the Colossians, to the Philippians, to Philemon. Paul sings no such joyful notes of praise as those which, in the Epistle to the Philippians, go soaring out of this very Roman imprisonment. It is as though God had given him, in the utmost way, his heart's desire.

That which is to be noted is, that his desire was given him *through the very things* which, at first sight, seemed to wear such hostile faces. Every one of them showed itself at last benignantly working together for his good. "And Paul dwelt two whole years in his own hired house, and received all that came unto him, preaching the kingdom of God, and teaching those things which concerned the Lord Jesus Christ, with all confidence, no man forbidding him."

Let *us* get grip on the mighty truth—*all things* do work together for *our* good, if we but love God. Here is ever-coming comfort.

THE MEN NEEDED.

I THINK Stephen is an example of them. He was a man possessing the courage of conviction. Of one thing he was sure—that Jesus was Messiah—gathering into substance and fulfillment all the shadowy and prophetic Mosaic past. Being sure, it was his duty to herald this evangel. It was not his to be discreet or polite about it. It was his to tell the immense truth out in all places and at any time. The Jewish Sanhedrim needed to know it as soon and as certainly as any. Standing there a prisoner before them, it was still his to tell them; and he does tell them calmly, lovingly, but with the strong courage which springs from an assured conviction. Whether the issue to him shall be life or death, it is his to be true to his Lord and to himself.

Martyrs like Stephen, in God's good providence, we need never be. The true faith has drawn the teeth of persecution in these days and in this land. But men like Stephen there is need that we now be and ought to be—men of convictions, men of the courage of convictions, men who will steadfastly bear their testimony.

The old Jewish Sanhedrim is dead long ago; but there are still other Sanhedrims, before which every man must be summoned. There are Sanhedrims of *unbelief*. Their council chambers are crowded just now thick about our lives. Many of those who call themselves the learned of the earth take their seats within them. They will tell you that your religion is a myth, a figment, a delusion. You will meet them in society. You will read their utterances too often in the daily press. They have a charmed word with which just now they fling their spell; that word is "liberal." He who can doubt the most is the man most liberal; and not to be liberal in their sense, in their thought, is to be mean and to be a fool. Well, the Lord needs before this modern Sanhedrim men of the courage of conviction; men who would rather be stigmatized as illiberal than yield their truth, or even allow that it is misty with perhapses; men to whom God, and the Bible, and the atoning Christ mean something; men who are ready to acknowledge in any presence, and under any circumstances, that they do carry the most awful and tremendous meanings. The need for Stephens is not yet done.

There is the Sanhedrim of *business*. Here, too, is needed the courage of conviction and brave witnessing—men who will say, in the presence of that Sanhedrim: "You may have your tricks of trade; you may have your questionable methods, through which the line between the wrong and right tremulously wavers; you may stain your hands with badly gotten gold, and call things, which ought to be designated wrong, only sharp and clever; but we are men who stand for the Lord Christ in bank and store and street, as well as in church on Sunday; and a bargain which we cannot make with the clear vision of his eye upon us is a bargain which we will not make, though you assure us it is swollen with millions for us, waiting to be brought to birth."

There is the Sanhedrim of the *family* and of *companionship*, before which the daily test is tried whether the mind which was in Christ Jesus shall be really the mind which is in us; whether we shall forget ourselves as he forgot himself; whether we shall be courageous with his love, and long suffering with his patience, and sweet and tender with his loveliness, and open handed with his charity.

And the Lord has need of Stephens still, who shall be true to him; who shall stand the testing; whose lives shall be significant for him; and who, though they may never be brought to die by stoning, as Stephen was, for Jesus' sake, shall yet be, for the sake of that same Jesus, courageous with the martyrdom of daily life in sick rooms and in toiling for the poor, and in the service of the Sunday-school, and along all the endless avenues of duty, thoughtless of self that they may remember him, and may cause others to remember him.

It shall not be needful that we die Stephen's death; but it is thoroughly needful that we do, in spirit and in deed, live Stephen's life of courageous faithfulness to Jesus. Such men are needed.

HOW TO BE A CHRISTIAN.

"I KNOW I am a sinner," he said. "I feel the burden of my sin. I want to be a Christian, but I don't know how to be. I am like a man feeling around in the dark. I don't know where to step."

"Do you believe that the Lord Jesus tells you the truth, and will never deceive you?" I asked.

"Certainly I do," he answered. "I haven't the slightest doubt about that."

"You are absolutely sure," I inquired, "that the Lord Jesus cannot lie?"

"Absolutely sure," he said.

"Well, now," I replied, "since you are so certain that Christ never can deceive you, why won't you take him exactly at his word? He tells you these words, 'Him that cometh unto me, I will in no wise cast out.' Now, coming is the yielding up of your sin, forsaking it, consecrating your soul to him. Don't you suppose that if you do your part of it, it is perfectly certain that Christ will do his part—receive you—never cast you out?"

"I think it must be so," he answered.

"Well, now," I asked again, "as far as you know yourself, do you thus come?"

He waited a minute, and then said solemnly:

"As far as I know myself, I do."

"Can you not, then," I answered, "just believe that promise, let your faith fasten on that word as a word for you, 'I will in no wise cast out'?"

There was absolute stillness for a moment, then the man looked up suddenly and exclaimed:

"Why, is that all?"

"That is all," I answered.

"Why," said he slowly, as if speaking to himself, "then—I think—I must be a Christian."

"My brother, you are a Christian," I answered joyfully.

Thus did this man become then and there a Christian.

Can we not all do thus and be saved?

Said James Durham, a minister in Glasgow, on his death-bed, to a friend:

"Brother, for all that I have preached and written, there is but one Scripture I can remember or dare to grip to. Tell me if I dare lay the weight of my salvation upon it. 'Him that cometh unto me, I will in no wise cast out.'"

"You may depend upon it, though you had a thousand salvations at hazard," was the answer.

That "*in no wise*" is a double negative: I will not, no, I will not cast out; and in whatever darkness, or sense of sinfulness, or agony of remorse, or out of whatever depth of evil, the soul coming to Christ lays grip to that, that soul is saved infallibly—and not life, nor death, nor angels, nor principalities, nor powers, nor things to come, nor height, nor depth, nor any creature, shall be able to separate that soul from the love of God which is in Jesus Christ our Lord. Coming and thus resting on his word, that is being a Christian. The personal contact with the personal Christ—that is true religion.

DIVINE LOVE.

OUTSIDE the Bible, you find revelation enough of law, but little of love. Some time since, looking out of my study window, I saw a blind man sitting on the stone steps opposite. I had often seen him led along the streets, picking up a living by peddling his little wares. Through the adaptation of our healthy eyes to the delicately smiting waves of the sunbeam, you and I get personal consciousness of the law of vision. Through the damage that has somehow come to that man's eyeballs, so that they are no more susceptible to the smiting sunbeams, that poor man gets sad personal consciousness of the *law* of want of vision. For him, there is but the blackness of darkness, whether the sun rise, or whether it set; but from no law of vision, or of the want of it, can you or he get knowledge of an Infinite and Beating Heart, which broods and yearns and blesses, in the light and in the darkness too; which in our affliction is itself afflicted; which seeks to pour the tides of an untiring affection round every creature; which opens itself for refuge to every struggler.

It is law there—healthy eyeballs and smiting sunbeams, and so vision; damaged eyeballs and smiting sunbeams, and never a glimmer of light, though the sun rise. But in the Bible you have an added revelation of the Infinite and Personal Love which, while it will not break law, will still use it for our help and blessing; which will even turn the darkness and the sorrow into ministry of spiritual and moral good.

Perhaps there are no Bible words which tell of this love better than the following: "Having loved his own which were in the world, he loved them unto the end." He loved them unto the end in this sense: that no hazard of personal cost whatever stopped the flowing of his love. When I was a boy, I used to read over and over again the story of a father and a mother and a child caught amid the New Hampshire mountains in a terrific snow-storm. The way was lost; the storm was blinding; the cold was bitter. Far in the distance, there was a gleam in a farm-house. The mother and the child could not go another rod, they were so exhausted. The father made for the distant light, to seek assistance; found it; brought it with him; found the child warm and living; found the mother stiff and dead; for she had, in the bitter cold, stripped herself of her own garments, to wrap them round the child. That mother, having loved her own, loved unto the end. In this sense exactly does the Divine Love keep flowing on. It stops at no cost whatever.

It stopped not at the cost of the incarnation. Then the Creator, as Mrs. Browning sings it,

> Was rent asunder from his first glory,
> And cast away on his own world.

Then Infiniteness circumscribed itself with finiteness. Then he who in the beginning was, and was with God, and was God, humbled himself, and became found in fashion as a man. To tell the meaning of that condescension, words fail, and human thought is as a laggard snail compared with the eagle's unhindered flight.

It stopped not at the cost of the temptation, when Divinity lowered itself to meet and master, in human weakness and temptability, the devil, who hounds men like a roaring lion, seeking whom he may devour.

It stopped not at the cost of an awful and mysterious contact with the sinfulness to which man had given himself. "Suppose," another says, in words most eloquent, "that the purest woman in this town, the most sensitive and scrupulous, moved by a sense of sisterhood, and by a loving pity, gathers up all her life, and goes and lives amid the lowest and the most brutal and the most foul savages that this world can contain. As she enters that life, she leaves her own life behind. She accepts their life; everything, except their wickedness, she makes her own. She sacrifices her fastidiousness every day. She finds herself the victim of habits which are the consequences of long years of sin. No sensibility that is not shocked; no fine, pure taste that is not wounded.

Her common human nature asserts itself every day; but the very depth of the union into which she comes with them by her pity, makes her all the more sensitive to the horror of their life. Their sin is awful to her, not only because of her own purity, but because of the keen understanding of its awfulness which comes from her profound oneness of nature with these sinners. She cannot stand far off, and look at them and work for them at a safe distance. She is one of them, in her common humanity. In every foul wickedness of theirs, she suffers. She bears their sins, a heavy burden, on her heart." May not such words as these aid our conception of what that suffering was, from the cost of which, through love of man, he held not back when he shared our nature and came into contact with its sin, and, shutting heaven's gates behind him, placed the feet of his purity upon this defiled earth of ours?

That Divine Love stopped not either at the cost of Calvary. It claimed the cross. It laid itself upon that world-atoning altar. It took man's place in the frowning presence of a violated law. It sundered itself from the Father's smile, which had been its life. It piled upon its shoulders the weight and penalty of human sin. It passed into that crisis of sacrifice, when Jesus cried: "My God! my God! why hast thou forsaken me?" It broke its heart. It died.

Nay, I am sure that that Divine Love stopped not, either, at the cost of a certain perpetual sacrifice for us; for I remember that that dip into human nature was not a transitory one for thirty-three brief years, and then a passage out of it. After the atonement had been accomplished, and the resurrection had set the seal of infinite victory and approval upon it, I remember that the Lord Christ did not shuffle off our human nature as something he had done with, and which could be left now to get on by its own forces. I remember that he did not rise into his own proper and absolute divinity, leaving us behind; but that he carried up into the glory with him our human nature; that he rose and ascended a man, as utterly as he was crucified a man; and that, now one with us still, he carries on the work of intercession for us. When he gave himself to us in the mystery of his incarnation, he gave himself to stay among us, to wear our nature forevermore, to be, unendingly, the incarnate Christ. He is Christ the glorified, indeed; but he is still Christ wearing the glorified human nature. Heaven robs him not of brotherhood with us; and whatever sacrifice Deity may have made when it embosomed itself in our nature, at least that sacrifice remains; for human nature glorified in Christ is human nature still. Do you not think of certain dim great words of Scripture? Precisely what they mean, I know not; but that they have some real, profound significance of loving sacrifice which, perhaps, eternity may disclose to us, I am sure: "A lamb slain from the foundation of the world." Unto such end, then, does the Divine Love go, pouring itself out upon us, that there is no rock of sacrifice in its path that it does not overflow and overwhelm, as tides do the pebbles on the beach.

But there is still another meaning which this expression, "unto the end," may hold. God not only loves men with a love which will go to the end of any sacrifice he must make, but he also loves them with a love which will go on until it has accomplished the end of his love in them, namely, their perfection. That is a poor thought of our religion which confines it simply to getting safely into heaven. It means much more. It means accurate conforming of our characters to the image of his Son. This love, purposing such an end, will not hesitate to use all the loving severity which may be needful to accomplish it, for there is in real love, necessarily, a certain side and element of severity. My child was studying her German lesson. It was tangled and difficult. The day was bright, and her mates were romping in the street. She wanted to miss the lesson and join the play; but, when she asked me if she might, my very love forced me to denial. I saw an end for her that she could not yet see—a present discipline she needed; a future grasp of mind and culture; the open gates of a mighty literature, into which this tangled lesson was the path. She might have thought I loved her more just then, if I had bidden her lay away her books and take her pleasant time; but a love which saw with larger, other eyes than hers the end, compelled the severity of denial. The parable is plain enough. Much that seems jagged in our lives is but the expression of God's pure love, working toward his end.

There is a sweet legend of the death of Moses in the Talmud. Three angels dig the grave upon the mountain, and Moses lies down in it, closes his eyelids, presses his hand upon his heart, and places his feet in order. Then the Lord calls to the soul to come forth and mount to Paradise. But the soul has not courage to go. Then he promises a place in the highest heaven, beneath cherubim and seraphim, who bear up the eternal throne; but still the soul doubts and quakes. Then God bent over the face of Moses and kissed him; and the soul leaped up in joy, and went forth with the kiss of God to Paradise. So does God's love brood over us and variously entice us, that, at last, we may be lifted to himself. We make our own doom if we withstand it.

MORAL DISINCLINATION.

WE are told in the Old Scriptures that the children of Manasseh could not drive out the inhabitants of those cities, but the Canaanite would dwell in the land. As the children of Israel then were, they could not—that was true enough; for they were in no mood for engaging in a decisive struggle. They preferred ease to energy. Josephus tells us they had grown effeminate.

Also, lapped in luxury, and thinking more of their own pleasant ease than of their nobler duty, these Israelites had lost pure and prevailing faith in God. Ceasing to fight in accordance with God's command, of course they had ceased to conquer; and ceasing thus to use Jehovah's promise of victory, of course they had ceased to find his promise actual to themselves in the further struggles they ought to undertake, but did not. And so, letting the weapon of their faith rust in a bad non-use, they could not drive out these Canaanites from their strongholds.

Also, lying thus in their enervating ease, and losing thus their pure faith in God, the dangers and difficulties in the way of the extirpation of these Canaanites were to their thought correspondingly increased. The strongholds, to their fearful, ease-loving feeling, grew very strong; the fortress perched upon the rocky hill-tops, seemed very unassailable; the chariots of iron, which, drawn by maddened horses, and horrible with long, sharp knives, would come dashing down upon their ranks, grew awfully terrible.

So, looked at from the side of their enervated hands, and weakened faith, and exaggerated difficulty, it is true that the children of Manasseh could not drive out the inhabitants of those cities; and so it would certainly be true that the Canaanites would dwell in that land.

But think, now, of these Israelites marshaled and armed for their duty; think of them as determined to obey God's command; think of them as ready to put Jehovah to the proof, and to go forth, risking themselves on his promise. Then, certainly, the *could not* would have belonged to the Canaanites. Then there had been written another sort of Scripture, like this: " And the children of Manasseh *would* drive out the inhabitants of those cities, and the Canaanites *could not* dwell in that land."

So we come to this fact about the mood of these Israelites—that the *could not* means really *would not;* that the real reason of their inability was a deep-seated moral disinclination. This moral disinclination—at the heart, will not; on the lip, cannot—is the commonest excuse men offer for not winning the moral triumphs they know they ought.

It is the commonest excuse of *damaged men.* Now and then, you see advertisements for the sale of damaged goods — goods drenched by water, smoked by fire, worn by shop-wear—good for something, but not good for much. Damaged goods have their counterpart in damaged men. What bright, promising boys many of them were! How fondly paternal and maternal eyes saw high visions of their future! How full, standing there on life's threshold, they seemed of lifted purpose, of grand courage, of ability to be and do! Sweet, generous, noble impulses seemed to sway them. Perhaps some trusting woman has yielded them herself in marriage; perhaps little children hail them father, and climb upon their knees. But the world has not used them well, they say. Somehow, where other men have gotten up, they have gone gradually but surely down. A mist has fallen on their prospects. They are in a fog, and they must stay in it. Things go well with other men; nothing goes well with them. They had friends; but their friends now walk, almost always, on the other side the street. They had chances; but the gates of fate have been shutting up their chances one by one. They had a pleasant home; but home is not what it used to be. An east wind is blowing through the house; frost is nipping the household flowers; nothing grows well there; they like the street or the club better. Once I tried to climb up a steep river bank, the sides of which were formed of a loose and comminuted shale. I sunk my feet into the soft shale and started. I got up a little way. Then it was as if the whole bank began to go down with me. I went on, but was carried down. As the larger stones became dislodged, I had continually to dodge them. It was hard, discouraging climbing. So life looks to these damaged men. When they try to get up a little way, at once they seem to themselves to be carried down. "Going to the bad," men say of them. Why? Let another tell the reasons: "The spell of evil companionship; the willingness to hold and use money not honestly gained; the stealthy, seductive, plausible advances of the appetite for strong drink; the treacherous fascinations of the gaming table; the gradual loss of interest in business and in things which help a man up; the rapid weakening of all moral purpose; the decay of manliness; the recklessness and blasphemy against fate; the sullen despair of ever breaking the chains of evil habit." These things, and things like these, are in the heads and hearts of these damaged men.

Now, go to them and tell them that, though—as in their better moments they will themselves confess—they are damaged, there is no need that they stay so. Tell them, if they will but go forth against these evil Canaanites, if they will but break off their sins by righteousness, if they will but let themselves be girded by the strength of Christ, they may yet win a noble victory—pass into a strong, self-respecting, and respect-compelling manhood. Tell them that the blood of Jesus Christ, his Son, cleanses the past and is energy for the days to come. Urge them, persuade them, promise them your own friendship, that you will gladly lay yourself out in any way to lift them from the blight of damage into the clear, sweet consciousness of the right. Too sad, often this will be their answer: "Oh, I would, but I cannot; I have tried and failed, and so I am sure I cannot." Ask them to say they will, and they will ever dodge you, replying: "I will try." With a real volition they will not go forth. They know in their deepest heart, if they would, they could, putting up weak, human hands that the divine hand may clasp their own. Their trouble is the Israelitish trouble. It is as modern as it is ancient. Their trouble is moral disinclination. Their *cannot* means *will not*. They do not like altogether their damaged plight. There are many unpleasant things about it. There must be. There must always be. God never can make sin blessed. But they do prefer even this state of damage, and what belongs to it, to the real, regular strain and wrench of will which is the first and inexorably needful step of the getting out of it. Toward that there is a terrible moral disinclination, and so they go on sighing, "I cannot," when the tremendous fact about it is they will not.

This moral disinclination—at the heart, will not; on the lip, cannot—is also the commonest excuse of merely moral men. It would not be right to call them damaged. They are not.

They are fair, square, prosperous, reputable men. They are honored in society, and they should be. Their home is safe beneath the benign shadow of their fame. They are clean in habit. They are, as the world goes, above reproach.

But a captain in the army once said to Uncle John Vassar:

"I try to do my duty; I think that is all that is required of me."

"Why, captain, how can you say so?" answered Uncle John. "No man does his duty who does not give his heart to God and live in God's service. What would you think of a man, brought up by a kind father, and provided by him with every kind of happiness, who should be a good brother and husband and neighbor and citizen, and yet be a heartless and undutiful son? Do you not see his wickedness would be unspeakably great?"

"But the cases are different," he replied.

"No, they are not," said Uncle John; "that man would be condemned by the moral sense of the community; and the godless sinner, you may depend upon it, will be condemned by the moral opinion of the universe."

It is strange how men will go on in a morality which is all right as far as it goes, but which can never go far enough, because it stops this side of the heart yielded to him who has a right to say, "My son, give me thine heart." But this moral man, who has heard the gospel for many a year, wakes now and then to a consciousness that his heart ought to be given. But that would involve making a new centre for his life. That would apply to it new standards —not, What do my neighbors think about things? but, What does God think about things? That would necessitate wrenching out of the groove of comfortable moral habit. So this man often says, "I cannot," but means "I will not." "I cannot" is the faint excuse. Moral disinclination is the genuine hindering cause. Let us beware of a cannot which is really will not. These Israelites were not the less guilty, muttering their false cannots.

INCREASE.

WRITES Paul to the Thessalonians—"I beseech you, brethren, that ye increase more and more."

So, then, the spiritual life, in the thought of Paul, was nothing stationary. It was something growing. It was something increasing. And Paul's thought was Christ's thought too. In the grounds of the palace of Hampton Court, near London, there is a wonderful grape vine. It is a black Hamburgh vine. It is more than a hundred years old. Nor for all that time has it ceased growing, and burdening itself yearly with numerous clusters. The year I saw it, that single vine had twelve hundred and fifty clusters hanging from its branches. Under its shade, and looking up at this wealth of fruitage, the words of the Lord Jesus came to me with strange significance: "Herein is my Father glorified, that ye bear much fruit. So shall ye be my disciples." Life, fruitage, going on to fruitage, increase, this was the thought of our Lord Jesus, for the spiritual life, as well as the thought of Paul. Decrease—that is not the word for the spiritual life. Standing still, merely holding one's own—that is not the word for it. Increase—that is the word for it.

Now I imagine that on this point of increasing more and more, the experience of many Christians is especially dim and misty, and unsatisfactory. They have a very much more conscious and definite experience of the beginning of the spiritual life, than they have of its advance. The beginning was something definite. The subsequent advance is too much indefinite. They have an uncomfortable, vague, straining feeling that they ought to get on; but they cannot feel much that they are getting on. Indeed, the faces of many are turned backward toward the vigor and brilliance of a first love, not forward toward the stronger strength and nobler shining of a better and a deeper love. Indeed, many are conscious of a certain real inward deterioration. They know their prayers are less prayerful, their consciences less quick, their spiritual purposes less stringent and less girded, their soul life in a state of sleep and winter, rather than in a state of growth and fruit-bearing and summer. And some who will not confess themselves in such a state of spiritual decadence are nevertheless really in it. The prophet Hosea had a lengthened ministry. He had fallen on sad times. Evil of every sort was rampant in the land. Plot, and treachery, and conspiracy dethroned king after king, and the wickedness of the rulers was but the bloom of the wickedness striking through the people. All the signs pointed, not toward national advance, but toward national extinction. And yet the people were all unconscious of their decaying state; and that was the saddest feature—that they were unconscious of it. What could save them if they would not be waked up to save themselves? So this is Hosea's sad description of them: "Gray hairs are here and there upon him, yet he knoweth not." The deterioration is all the time going on, and yet Israel is ignorant of it. That is true of many a church and many a soul to-day—not increasing more and more, but unconscious spiritual deterioration.

So, then, what I propose to do just now is to look at our Scripture by way of contrast; not to urge the duty of spiritual increase—there were no need of that, that is confessed already; but to seek to point out, if I may, some of the causes which prevent a spiritual advance.

Roughly, man is analyzed into three great energies. He is a being possessing *thought, affection, will.* For the sake of clearness, let us use this large and real analysis.

Let us think of some of the causes preventing spiritual increase in the realm of the thought, in the realm of the affection, in the realm of the will.

In *the realm of the thought,* a common cause preventing increase in the spiritual life is, the failure to thoughtfully discriminate, under the light of the teachings of the Master, between really right feeling and action and their counterfeits. Let me illustrate my meaning: The Duke of Argyle tells us "that there are many species of the genus mantis which are wholly modeled in the form of vegetable growths. The legs are made to imitate leaf-stalks, the body is elongated and notched so as to simulate a twig, the segment of the shoulders is spread out and flattened in the likeness of a seed-vessel, and the large wings are exact imitations of a full-blown leaf, with all its veins and skeleton complete, and all its color and apparent texture. There is something startling and almost terrible in the completeness of the deception—very terrible it must be to its hopeless victims. It is the habit of these creatures to sit upon the leaves which they so closely resemble, apparently motionless, but really advancing on their prey with a slow and insensible approach. Their resemblance disarms suspicion." So, as another has suggested, there are counterfeits in Christian deed and feeling. Decision is a Christian grace, but how easily it passes over into its counterfeit—a harsh and evil overbearingness.

Earnestness is a Christian grace, but how easily it passes over into its counterfeit—an unholy and, perhaps, even petulant *impatience*. Confidence is a Christian grace. It is both right and possible for the Christian to say I *know* whom I have believed, but how easily it passes over into its counterfeit—a vainglorious spiritual pride. Gentleness is a Christian grace, but how easily it passes over into its counterfeit—a poor and helpless *weakness*, which has no backbone about anything. Contentment is a Christian grace, but how easily it may pass over into its counterfeit—a stupid and sluggish indifference. Caution is a Christian grace, but how easily it may pass over into its counterfeit—a limp timidity. Boldness is a Christian grace, but how quickly may it get into its counterfeit—a careless rashness. There is room and reason for thoughtful, self-examining, prayerful discrimination here. It is so easy for the decided man to be overbearing, or the quieter man to be weak, or the earnest man to be impatient, or the bold man to be rash—and the failure to make such discrimination, you can easily see, is a failure to illustrate at once the sweetness and the power, the winningness and the stalwartness of the Christian life. The failure of our loyal reception into our thought of Christ's doctrines, and the failure of thoughtful and prayerful application of those doctrines to our own feelings and actions, are common causes, in this realm of the thought, which prevent increase in the spiritual life.

But notice a few of the causes preventing increase in the spiritual life in *the realm of the affections*. Now, in this realm, a great hindering cause is a leaving of the first love. The Church in Ephesus had many things which even Christ could praise: it had good works, it had activity, it had patience, it had protest against evil, it had doctrinal fidelity, it had unfainting energy; and yet it was failing and blameable, because it had not kept first that which was first—a supreme love to him who walketh amid the golden candlesticks. How could it help failing, failing here. What Coleridge says of love in the lower sense, is true even in the spiritual and higher:

> All thoughts, all passions, all delights,
> Whatever stirs this mortal frame,
> Are but the ministers of love,
> And feed its sacred flame.

If that flame fail, all these fail too.

"For, what is temperance," says an old writer, "but love which no pleasure seduceth; what is prudence, but love which no error enticeth; what is fortitude, but love which endureth adverse things with courage; what is justice, but love which composeth by a certain charm the inequalities of this life." But, if love go down, these go down with it, just as when the heart fails, life fails in brain and eye and limb. So there can be no such thing as increase in the spiritual life, if that love which should be first, be not kept first.

If a religious indifference be allowed to strike its chill over that fire, spiritual life must decline. As another says: "The Scythians used to strike the cords of their bows at their feasts, to remind themselves of danger. If we are intent against heaviness, it will flee away."

If a stupid desire for religious ease stop the draught for the flame of love, the spiritual life must flicker. If a contaminating, secular, and worldly spirit poison the air on which that love feeds, there can be neither health nor glow in the religious life.

And if some other love—the sad love for some sad sin—take the place of that supreme love on the heart's altar, how can love of sin, forcing out the pure love and the foremost, minister anything but damage and decay to the spiritual life?

Said one, amid the wilds of Australia, who had loved purely, and the fires of which love he would not let die out: "I was kept from many a sad sin simply by this thought: 'for her sake.'" And no Christian can possibly increase in the spiritual life who, amid life's duties and self-conflict and stringencies, is not gladly conscious of the moving of this overmastering motive in him, for Christ's sake.

Guard your love, if you would grow in grace. Let your soul get warmth from no alien flame, and refuse to have to do with anything which will not to the love of Christ bring fuel. Keep thine heart with all diligence, for out of *it* are the issues of life.

But notice, also, wnat cause there may be in *the realm of the will*, preventing increase in the spiritual life.

Mary Anne Clough was a factory girl in Glasgow. She worked with her own hands for her daily bread. She sped to the factory in the cold, dark mornings, long before half the world was up. She wrought on through the long hours, until the waning day had brought again the darkness. The Scotch factory children, in their ignorance and vice and squalor, began to trouble her as she mingled with them. She became full of a woman's and of a Christian's pity for them. She said, I will try if I can win them to God, and to doing what is good. Now, of course, it was a very right and gracious thing for Mary Clough to have such feelings. But do you not see that the feeling simply would neither have lifted her nor lifted them? There is even a certain selfish pleasure in tender and loving feeling simply. How many cry over novels, and yet are no better for their crying.

But Mary Clough did not stop at feeling; she turned her will into a channel for her feeling, and set her feeling flowing through her will and out to something. She got an empty room in the basement of the factory. On the Sundays and in the evenings of the toiling days, she gathered the factory children in it. She taught them, cleaned them, lifted them, loved them. Pretty soon there began to be sweet, clean, pure-minded children about the factories. Mary Anne's boys they were, the people said. Out of that small seed has grown, and is growing to-day, a mighty and permanent Christian charity, the Glasgow Foundry Boys' Religious Society. Now, do you not see how great a Christian was Mary Clough, and do you not see that she was lifted into such Christ-hood because she did not let feeling wait at the place of will, but through will took up that Christian feeling and carried it out and into Christian action?

Here, then, is a too common preventing cause

of increasing religious life. We are not enough like Mary Anne Clough. We too frequently baffle right feeling by bad and sluggish will, and so we waste it and soon kill it.

It is right feeling flowing out through right will into right action that ministers to grace, and makes strong and fruitful the spiritual life.

We do not need so much to feel more, as to transmute what we already feel into holy action by a holy will.

This is what Christians ought to be—like pictures showing deeper tints and lovelier colorings as the days go by—improving as they get older; like violins—scattering sweeter music the more the bow is drawn across them, singing in richer tones the harder they are put at service.

"THE SUNDAYS OF MAN'S LIFE."

IN one of the English coal mines, there is what the miners call a Sunday stone. Water charged with lime is trickling through the rocks, and, as it falls, is making constant deposits of pure white limestone. But when the miners are at work, and are scattering the coal-dust all about, the water becomes charged with coal as well as lime, and the stone, which otherwise were white, takes upon itself the black coal hue.

But when the Sunday comes, and the men cease working, and the whirring coal-dust settles, then upon the blackness of the deposit of the day before begins to drop the clean lime water, leaving, as it trickles off, the pure white stone. And so, by the regularly recurring line of whiteness, record is made of the coming to the tired miners of God's day of rest.

Into your tired lives comes, as well, the Sunday

whiteness. I know that some of you choose to stain it with the earthly dust you will not let lie quiet on God's Day. But that is your fault, not God's. Once a week, he gives you this white, protected day.

And when you count up what George Herbert sings of, as

> The Sundays of man's life,
> Thredded together on Time's string,

their amount is startling, if you will reckon it by your arithmetic. The young man who has reached the age of twenty years, has received from the hand of God nearly three solid years of Sundays. He who has reached the age of forty years, has received from the hand of God nearly six solid years of Sundays. The man who has reached the age of sixty years, has received from the hand of God nearly nine solid years of Sundays. Can it be true that we have no time to seek God in?

They mean much—these Sundays. The tempest of toil is hushed beneath their "Peace, be still!" The strain of life loosens itself a little.

Not for them, the hurry of the street and the scramble of the market. Not needfully, for the Lord's Day, the anchoring the thought to the humdrum tasks. As when ships, safe from the swellings and the buffetings of the ocean, ride quietly in some fair harbor, so on the restful Lord's Day may your soul find mooring. This is the day for higher and other thinkings. This is the day when the soul may close the windows which look out toward the earth, and open those which front toward heaven. This is the day for spiritual stimulation.

These "Sundays of man's life, Thredded together on Time's string"—these years of them, what have we done, what are we doing unto them all? A solemn question this.

SUCCESS.

I HAVE thought much of these words as affording a divine suggestion concerning success in life. They are the words Paul wrote to the Galatians. "But when it pleased God, who separated me from my mother's womb, and called me by his grace, to reveal his Son in me, that I might preach him among the heathen, immediately I conferred not with flesh and blood."

Here is Paul's statement of his divine devotement to his duty; of the divine empowering for his duty; of his subsequent way of doing his duty.

The devotement was from the beginning—God separated him to his great office and function, from his mother's womb; that he should carry on his apostleship was the divine meaning of his appearance in the world.

I am sure we are to understand that this devotement took into itself all influences of heredity, of external circumstances, of various and peculiar education. It was because Paul had such a mother and such a father—Hebrews of the Hebrews, and yet dowered with the great dignity of Roman citizenship; it was because he was born, not in the narrow ritualistically confining air of Palestine, but in the freer air of Tarsus in Cilicia, and where Jews would not so much think Gentiles pitiable dogs; it was because he had the ampler education of such a Gentile city, but, also, in his impressionable boyhood was brought up at Jerusalem, according to the straitest sect of his religion, a Pharisee, at the feet of Gamaliel,—that he could be at once so thoroughly a Jew, and, at the same time, stand in welcoming attitude toward the Gentile; that he could preach Christ so triumphantly among the Gentiles, commending to them a Messiah who, though he was Saviour of all the world, was yet a Jew.

Except Paul had been thus divinely separated

from his mother's womb, and had been surrounded with such circumstances, and had been touched by so much and such various culture, he could not have wrought in and wrought through such an apostleship. God's hand was in it all.

The divine empowering for his duty was the revelation within himself of the personal Christ, " who called me by his grace, to reveal his Son in me."

It was because Paul knew Christ as his own personal Saviour, so intimately and so thoroughly, that he could preach him so enthusiastically and so conqueringly. Paul spoke out of an inward conviction; he knew whereof he affirmed, for he had felt it all, and mightily, in his own soul.

Paul's way of doing his duty was the way of simple personal loyalty to Christ: "Immediately I conferred not with flesh and blood."

The question was not what others thought, not what others said, but what, as far as he could find it out, the Lord Jesus would have him do.

The standard was not custom, not tradition, not example of other people, of other apostles, even; but the word of Christ as it had shone gloriously on him.

The divine separation to it, and the divinely arranged culture for it; the presence of the personal Christ in his personal soul; unwavering and inextinguishable personal loyalty to that Christ—these were the three vital roots of that magnificent apostleship.

I suppose that in the proportion in which these three roots are vital in any life, is that life genuinely successful.

When a man believes that God has given him something definitely to do in this world—whatever it be, whether merchandising, banking, farming, building, bricklaying, school teaching, pleading, healing, preaching; when a man receives into himself the high inspiration of religion for the doing of that thing; when a man holds himself in burning and pulsating loyalty primarily to the Great Task-master—then, I suppose, that man is likeliest to achieve at least what God will crown as a genuine success.

THE INNER SPRING.

THERE is a wonderful truth, veiled and yet evident, in the fourth verse of the Forty-sixth Psalm: "There is a river, the streams whereof shall make glad the City of God, the Holy Place of the tabernacles of the Most High." The Psalm is a burst of praise for the sudden and surprising deliverance from the beleaguring Sennacherib.

It was a very marked peculiarity of Jerusalem, it was a feature singular to it among the then cities of the world. Jerusalem was an altogether inland city. It was perched upon its hills amid surrounding mountains. It laved its feet in no broad river. It had no harbor looking outward on the sea. And yet no city was supplied with water as Jerusalem was, *within itself*. For there was within Jerusalem a living spring beneath the Temple vaults. It was this spring whence the water welled to fill the two Siloam pools. It was of this perennial spring, within Jerusalem, whence came the streams that made glad God's city, of which the Psalmist sings. "All my springs are in thee," bursts forth another Psalm. "Draw water out of the wells of salvation," exclaims Isaiah, referring to this unwasting internal fountain. It was the figure borrowed from this spring which Jesus used, when, there in the Temple, during the Feast of Tabernacles, he stood forth and cried: "If any man thirst, let him come unto *me* and drink; he that believeth on me, as the Scripture saith, out of him shall flow rivers of living water; but this spake he of the Spirit, which they that believe on him should receive."

So you see how strong and wonderful the figure really is. Sennacherib might come forth with countless armies, and bid them encamp about Jerusalem as locusts do, in thickening swarms. He might do many things. But there was one thing he could not do. He could not cut off Jerusalem from this internal and plentiful supply of clear, sweet water. The fountains of that were within herself. So far forth she could never be the slave of hostile circumstances; she was always the mistress of them.

Now, this will be the peculiar gift of God to us, if we will have it so—this of the inner spring. Even as Jesus said, speaking of the Holy Spirit, "He that believeth on me, out of him shall flow rivers of living water." God will thus be *in a man*, internal supply and strength; making him the sovereign of difficult circumstances, and not the thrall of them; making him possessed of something *within* himself which nothing outward can reach or drain away, even as Jerusalem, with this living spring welling up abundantly within herself, could not be forced to thirst even by the mighty armies of Sennacherib. Here is *abundant* supply of internal invigoration; for, as the Psalm says, this inward spring wells up, not into *a* stream simply, but into *streams*. Here is the fountain of the deepest and most unwasting joy; for, as the Psalm sings again, these streams *make glad* the city of God; and, after all, what gladness is comparable with the consciousness that God is, like the spring within Jerusalem, at the centre of one's life, feeding and filling one with an independent and unconquerable energy?

That is a poor life which has no resource in itself. It is the privilege of the Christian to have resource in himself. The Book of Acts is the record of the shaking of the world by the early Christians. With circumstances all against them, they, notwithstanding, shook the world. They shook the world, because they were conscious of an internal power. They were conscious of an internal power, because God dwelt in them by the Holy Spirit. It is a most significant fact that, in the Book of Acts, which is the record of power, the Holy Spirit is mentioned oftener than in any other book of Scripture; is mentioned no less than *seventy-one* separate times. It was because they had this river, the streams whereof make glad the city of God, so consciously within themselves, that those early Christians became, not poor and passive recipients of outward influences, but batteries of holy force.

How splendidly independent of outward circumstances this having God within one, by the indwelling of the Holy Spirit, can make a man.

As I have been reading lately, there was Cicero, exiled, but exiled with every mitigation; not imprisoned, simply exiled; he could live where and how he pleased; sumptuous house; troops of friends; luxurious table; abundant wealth—but, though he was philosopher and orator, filling his letters from his exile with unmanly whining. His life was rooted too much in circumstances, and when these failed, he failed.

Seneca, exiled; full of profession of a grand and stoical sovereignty over pain and passion; with the whole range of the island of Sardinia; with immense wealth; vast reputation; powerful in friends; but so struck down and subdued by his short exile that, like a whipped cur, he groveled at the feet of the worst of men, that his exile might cease. His life was rooted too much in circumstances, and when these failed, he failed.

But read the Epistle to the Philippians. It was written from a prison worse than exile. It was written where chains clanked, and poverty intruded, and death threatened. But peace reigns in it, and Psalms sing in it, and an unwasting joy shines in it. As a great commentator says of it: "The whole letter bears the impress, at times almost elegiac, of resignation in view of death; with high, apostolic dignity, unbroken holy joy, hope, and victory over the world." The apostle here, in his Roman imprisonment, as another so well says, "recalls to our mind the runner who, at the supreme moment of Grecian history, brought to Athens the news of Marathon. Worn, panting, exhausted with the effort to be the herald of deliverance, he sank in death on the threshold of the first house which he reached with the tidings of victory, and sighed forth his gallant soul in one great sob, almost in the very same words as those used by the apostle, 'χαίρετε χαίρομεν—Rejoice ye, we too rejoice.'" What was death to the runner, with such a joy as the victory of Marathon welling in his heart? What was the worst imprisonment to Paul, with the joy of the conscious indwelling of the God of power and the God of promise, by the Holy Spirit furnishing him with inward and holy and conquering vigor, whatever might betide?

Ah! this is the privilege of the Christian. There are for him internal springs. And how, amid the numerous and mighty Sennacheribs of various sorrows and evils crowding round our souls, do we need this divine indwelling, which shall be to us an internal fountain of invigoration, as was that internal river, the streams whereof made glad the city of God to the sorely beleaguered, but, because of this internal upwelling spring, still resistant and still triumphant Jerusalem.

GOD'S METHOD.

THIS has always seemed to me a luminous illustration of the divine triumph over evil in us and for us,—"And the God of peace shall bruise Satan *under your feet* shortly." In his autobiography, Dr. Lyman Beecher tells us that when he was pastor at East Hampton, there were a few Indians of the Montauk tribe connected with his parish. There was a pious squaw who used to come up when they were killing things before Thanksgiving, and gather scraps from the portions which were thrown away. She was picking round Colonel Gardner's barn.

"Come here, Betty," says Colonel Gardner—and packed her basket full of good solid meat, and handed it to her.

She looked up in silent astonishment. She could not believe her eyes. At last she lifted up her hands and said:

"Thank the Lord for giving me this meat. Thank you, too, Colonel Gardner."

The poor old Indian woman put it truly. God helped her, but he helped her through the Colonel. God wrought for her, but through second causes.

It is thus that God works for us and in us. God shall bruise Satan; but *under our own feet.* We are not merely passive recipients of the victory that God achieves. There must be in us the strong arm and the persistent battle. Out of temptations resisted, out of triumphs won, out of constant spurnings of the wrong, gradually rises and towers the stately character.

> I count this thing to be grandly true,
>   That a noble deed is a step toward God,
>   Lifting the soul from the common sod
> To a purer air and a broader view.
>
> We rise by things that are under our feet,
>   By what we have mastered of good and gain.
>   By the pride deposed and the passion slain,
> And the vanquished ills that we hourly meet.
>
> Heaven is not reached at a single bound;
>   But we build the ladder by which we rise
>   From the lowly earth to the vaulted skies;
> And we mount to its summit round by round.

Yet it is God who works for us, and in us, and yet still by us. We could gain no victory but in his strength. He must bruise Satan. Satan is too mighty for our feeble feet. But we can, by inward consecration, make alliance with the mighty One, and so find even Satan weak and bruised beneath our heel.

GRIEVING THE SPIRIT.

SENECA has left the world, and yet Seneca lives in it—a real force and influence, through the truth and beauty of many of the moral precepts he enunciated, universal to all men and all time.

Charlemagne has left the world, and yet he lives in it—a real force and influence, through the civilization which sprang out of his compelling that incoherent Europe into the organism of a single empire.

Newton has left the world, and yet he lives in it—a real force and influence, through the impulse he gave to science, by that grand generalization in which he rose to the conception of the all-including law of gravitation.

Milton has left the world, and yet he lives in it—a real force and influence, through the high argument of that mighty poem, in which he sought to justify the ways of God to men.

And so multitudes of others—orators, poets, statesmen, philanthropists, artists, whose names men will not willingly let die—have left the world, and yet are in it still, pervasive and present forces, through the stirring words they spoke, the noble songs they sang, the civilizations they inaugurated, the beneficence they planned, the pictures they painted.

So, too, Christ has left the world—not by death, as these have, but by glorious resurrection and ascension—and he too yet lives in the world. But how? Only as these live in it? Only in the way of the natural effects of his great historical appearance?

No! In a way as different from that in which all these abide among us, as is the actual presence of your friend from the poor memory of that friend after death has summoned you to the long farewell from him. How, then, does Christ still live among us? Let a story tell us.

Many years ago, a poor slave woman, who

could not read a line, who had struggled and wrestled toward God, darkened and oppressed with the agony of a great seeking, had revealed to her a vision of Jesus. It was to her a strange, new, wonderful revelation. She saw one standing between God and man, one who loved, and one who loved her. She felt that he loved her, and this knowledge poured a flood of light and joy into her heart. She said :

"I felt such a rush of love; I loved everything. I said, 'Yes, Lord, I ken love even the white folks.' But," she said, "I thought to myself, ef the white folks knows I've got Jesus, they'll get him away, somehow; and so I kep' it all to myself, and thought I wouldn't tell nobody. But," she continued, "I went to a Methodist class-meeting, and they began to get up and 'late their experiences. Well, the first one that spoke began to tell about Jesus. 'Why,' says I, 'that one has got him too.' And then another got up, and says I, 'He has got him too.' And finally says I, 'They's all got him.'"

This experience of the devout negro, and of

those to whom her heart could not help responding as she heard them speak of the Lord Jesus, is an experience peculiar and true of Christ only. It is possible to speak of knowing Christ by some spiritual intuition, of seeing Christ, of feeling Christ. Thus, divinely, intimately, really, not vaguely and remotely in the way of a general historic influence, but in veritable and personal presence—does Christ live in the world, in the hearts of those who love him. They have him.

But now, since Christ, in bodily presence, has ascended to the right hand of the Father, it is by the ministry of the Holy Spirit that he is thus present in the hearts of the believers.

The Holy Spirit dwelling in a man, is the divine Christ personally present in him.

But Christ is thus personally present in us only as we distinctly choose to have him thus. "The kingdom of God is within you." If we would have this kingdom of God within us, God our Lord Jesus dwelling in us thus, the Holy Spirit must be King. Everything must obey him. He must be absolute ruler. Hence the reason for the admonition of the Scripture that we "resist not," "limit not," "grieve not," "provoke not," "vex not," "quench not," the Holy Spirit. For what is doing any one of these things? It is choosing against Christ, and so dethroning Christ from our inner hearts.

THE FADING LEAF.

I SOMETIMES think that God has set the yearly time of decay amid such gorgeousness, that, while we may not fail to learn the sad and somber lessons, we may be enticed into deeper study, to reach the more hidden, but brighter and more hopeful truths, which it is given to the fading leaves to teach.

Here is a lesson the fading leaf may teach on its brighter side: That since we must fade, *we ought not to fade before our time.* While the leaf fades, it has its time for fading. It does not fade before its time. A sudden whirlwind may tear it off, but then it falls green, not faded. Sudden and early death may strike us too; but then we should die really young, not old and faded and worn-out, though young in years. Every leaf has its time to fade. Henry D. Thoreau—that man who lived a recluse life so many years in a hut, by the side of that small inland lake near Concord, and who had one of the keenest and most patient eyes that were ever opened upon nature—could tell to the very day, and almost to the very moment, when the leaves of the forest trees around him, oak, maple, chestnut, would begin to change and fade. While we do fade like the leaves, like them also we are not to fade before our time.

There is many a fresh young life eaten up and shriveled by some blight, long before its legitimate fading time. We call it a dispensation of Providence. I fear me, it is oftener really a dispensation of unwise parents, or of thick-headed and cold-hearted schoolmasters, or of ungoverned and passionate self-will, or of a wearing and wasting toil, or of thin dresses and thin shoes, amid the wintry air of some fashionable season.

Why! I have stood upon the street and seen the children coming home from school, too often wearing pale and weary faces, with laggard gait, with feverish appearance, going home to what?

—to play and rest, as they have a right, with never a thought more of books till the school-bell shall ring next morning? No; out of long hours of study at school, going into long hours of study at home—five and six lessons to learn a day (no child ought to learn more than three at the utmost). And then everybody, parents, teachers, friends, praising them for precocity; parents proud of the fact that their children will graduate so young; and the children robbed of their life, fading like the leaf in early summer, bitten by the worm or smitten by the blight.

So I have seen young men old men, and young women old women, because stimulants and dissipation of various sorts had been eating at them.

So, too, the blight of *hard and unceasing toil* causes many a fair young life to fade before its time. We cannot stand the strain of a constant toil, if it be real and honest. It is like keeping a leaf in the glare of the sun all the time, with no night to wrap it around with its dampness and its rest. Every toilful life must freshen itself; must fight off fading by rest.

I met some time ago an article from one of the world's most helpful living teachers, none the less so because she is a woman. It told how, in the old times, when children were more strictly ruled, Saturday afternoon was the children's perquisite. Then they did what they pleased; at other times, they did as they were bid. And so this writer tells us, every one should have a Saturday afternoon; when toil shall no more command, but rather, pleasure delightfully allow. No life can help fading without such a rest, any more than a leaf can keep green without rain. It makes little difference what that restful pleasure be, so long as it be right and restful, and a pleasure.

I remember how once, when I was in Nantucket, I went to see a cabinet of all sorts of incongruous curiosities, which one of the inhabitants of that quaint place was fond of showing. It had been picked up in all quarters of the world, by her husband, who had been a sailor. Almost everything was in it; but everything was carefully kept, and upon everything was hung a story—and such a bright, fresh, cheery, young old woman to show it, and to talk about it, as you rarely see. That cabinet had been her Saturday afternoon. It had been full of restful interest to her; it had held her in her affection for her husband, these things which *he* brought home. It had kept her young and fresh; it had fought off fading, and largely conquered it. She was fading as the leaf fades, gloriously in its time. Since we must fade, let us do it as the leaf does, and as God would have us, in the time of fading, not before. Let us use life as if it were a gift from God; not as abusing it, but as preserving it; then our decline shall be like the sun setting, companioned with radiant clouds, or like the autumn leaf, fading, but brighter in the colors of its decease than in the colors of its prime.

Here, too, I think, is another lesson on this brighter side from the fading leaves. Leaves fade and fall, *but only when their work is done: and their work remains.* Here is a stalk or branch with the young leaves of the early spring just budded out upon it. Wait till the autumn comes, and look at that branch again. The leaves are now fading on it, and falling from it, but, there is *piled upon its end a whole season's longer growth, and everywhere it is thicker through.* Why? Because each leaf upon that branch, all the season long has been paying a small tax to that branch for its sustaining. Each leaf, from the moment of its majority, collects for that branch a certain quantity of wood, or what will become wood, and sends it down the stalk, to add to its length and thickness; down the stalk; down further still, to the branch; to the tree-stem; to the most distant rootlet mining in the darkness. So is the whole tree stronger and larger for a single leaf. It is very little that the leaf does. It is only a slender filament of woody fiber, which the leaf sends down; but it has not failed; it has done its little well and wisely. Its work remains. Let it fade and fall, now that its work is done. Its death, that is only the signal of accomplishment and victory. So are the mighty forests builded by the patient, plodding working of the fading and the falling leaves. Nothing but leaves have built the forests up.

You may be fading, O my brother. You see with a dimmer sight; you step with a less elastic tread; you remember with a feebler grasp; you think with a slower brain. Well, these are only prophecies of victory, if your work has been bravely going on. Now the long struggle of the battle is drawing towards its end. Now the glory of the triumph begins to shine. It is into the lap of the fading autumn that is emptied the gathered richness of the year. The tasks of life are almost done. The leaf may fade and fall, but the work remains. The great Tree of Humanity is being lifted by the working of all these fading and falling leaves of men and women, clinging for a little to its branches. Says John Ruskin: "If ever in autumn, a pensiveness falls upon us, as the leaves drift by us in their fading, may we not wisely look up in hope to their mighty monuments? Behold how fair, how far, prolonged in arch and aisle the avenues of the valleys, the fringes of the hills! So stately, so eternal! The joy of man, the comfort of all living creatures, the glory of the earth, they are but the monuments of those poor leaves that flit faintly past us to die. Let them not pass except we understand their last counsel and example, that we also, careless of a monument by the grave, may build it in the world—a monument by which men may be taught to remember, not where we died, but where we lived."

Leaves fade and fall; but *that is not the end of it.* The winter comes with its wind to whirl them afar, and with its snows to bury them; but that is not the end of it. The faded fallen leaf is buried; but it is not lost. The leaf is scattered into soil at the tree's base; but it is not lost. Death is the slave of life. Life strikes its roots downward into death. That very fallen leaf transmuted into nutriment for the tree, shall be lifted up its trunk again, and be flung out a fresh banner from its topmost bough. Leaves fade and fall into death, but also, through death, into *another life.*

Oh, friends, a human fading may be but the beginning of the birth-process into the infinitely rich and restful life of heaven.

CHRIST AND THE GRAVE.

THERE is a sad, suggestive monument in Mount Auburn Cemetery, near Boston. There is a statue of a dog lying on its master's grave. The story of the statue is—that the master died; that the dog followed the dead body to the grave; that when the gravel had fallen upon the coffin in the grave, the dog lay down upon it; that nothing could induce the pitiful, loving creature to leave the spot; that what little food it ate of what was plentifully brought to it, it ate there upon that grave; that it hopelessly pined away; that soon it died; that then they dug a grave beside its master's for the faithful creature, and commemorated its devotion, as was fitting, by this statue. It is a sad statue, because it tells of such a dumb, hopeless sorrow. That was all the dog could know—that its master had been put there, under the ground. That was all the dog could do, to show its poor, pitiful, longing love—stay there, in a determined tenderness, until it died. You could not make the dog know anything more than that, anything higher. You could not tell the dog of any final certainty of immortality for the master he loved in such a dumb, devoted way. You could not make him understand the thought of heaven, and glorified being, and infinitely better life and destiny into which it was possible that master passed. All the dog could know was that they had put his master down there, under the ground, and that was the end of everything for the poor creature. It is a sad statue, because it is one that tells of sad, hopeless, unillumined, utterly disastrous sorrow falling down upon that to the last clinging and almost human affection.

The statue is significant, for it is to just such darkened, despairing sorrow that much of the modern thinking would lead us. For that, there is nothing that tells of certain and sufficient light beyond death. Robert Ingersoll, with breaking heart and manly tears, seeking to say something over the coffin of his dead brother, can say scarcely more than this dog could have said, had he been gifted with the ability of speech. For him, there is no certainty, no sunrise; at best, but the vanishing flutter of the faintest hope. The pagan thought of death was only that of this poor, dumb dog, lying here on his master's grave. "She who lies here, coveted not, while alive, garments of gold, but desired discretion and virtue; but now, Dionysia, in place of youth and bloom, the fates have awarded thee this sepulchre." So reads a recently disinterred Athenian burial inscription. It is the sorrow of the poor, dumb creature. There is the sepulchre—that is all there is. Take your modern thinking which declares itself to be the rational and scientific; what does it bring men to but just the hopeless sorrow of this despairing animal? There was John Stuart Mill. If ever a man loved his wife, he did his. If ever a woman loved her husband, sympathizing with him in his work, sharing with him in his studies, refusing to let him go alone, but keeping pace with him with equal footstep, she loved John Stuart Mill. So, naturally enough, an increasing and intelligent and unwasting love bound them together. She died; and at once a light went out of the heart and life of the great thinker. "Since then," says Mr. Mill, "I have sought for such alleviation as my state admitted of, by the mode of life which most enabled me to feel her still near me. I bought a cottage as close as possible to the place where she is buried, and there her daughter and I live constantly during a great portion of the year." I say it with reverence and with sadness, but what is that but the poor dog lying on his master's grave? Not a word of brighter or better hope than that could John Stuart Mill's way of thinking let him say.

No certainty of existence, of a richer life, of a grander destiny beyond. That grave ended everything; that grave was the end of everything. Into that grave they had put *her* he loved—not the body, not the external tabernacle in which she dwelt here, but *her;* as for anything beyond, he could know nothing; he could hope nothing. It knows much, it says; it can talk learnedly about atoms fortuitously concoursing; it can put force and law in the place of God; it can scorn the Bible as a mass and mess of old wives' fables; but this is where it brings you—this vaunting modern science of the material—to such sorrow as that dog had lying on its master's grave, and dying there itself, because it could not know but that they had laid him there—the whole of him.

But now there is a great and undeniable and historic fact which, if we will but see it, puts light and certainty and a divine and celestial sun on the other side that grave. For darkness there is radiance; for death there is life. They hung Christ on that cross. They did it in the eyes of the assembled multitudes. It was no out of the way execution. Not alone did the Jews do it either. The Romans had a hand in it. The Jewish Sanhedrim condemned, but the Roman Pilate executed. It was he who gave commandment, as publicly as official could, that he be crucified. They crashed the nails through hands and feet. They thrust the spear-head into his inmost heart. He was dead; there could be no doubt about it. He could not have swooned. He could not have been smitten with a syncope. No man ever lived with his heart cleft. The Roman soldiers certified his death. The Jewish rulers certified his death. Pilate, in the chair of the proconsul, certified his death.

They put him in a sepulchre. It was no old tomb in which multitudes of dead had lain. It was not possible that another be mistaken for him. This Christ was that tomb's first and lonely occupant. It was a new tomb, in which never before had a dead body found a resting-place.

They marked that tomb; the disciples marked it with their love; the Jewish Sanhedrim marked it with their hate; the Roman government marked it with their watching. They rolled a great stone to that tomb's mouth. They sealed it with that Roman seal, to disturb which brought the disturber death. They set sentinels, pacing back and forth before that tomb. There could be no mistake about it—that was the tomb. Into that tomb had he been carried who died upon that cross. It is not so certain that Napoleon was beaten at Waterloo as that this Christ was nailed to that cross, and was dead when they took him down with a spear gash in his heart, and was placed in that new and sealed and guarded sepulchre.

Wonderful the precautions which they took against possible mistake. All unwittingly, you say. True, God's hand was in it. He makes the wrath of man to praise him, the remainder he restrains. But if anything is historically certain, this is. Friends the most loving, enemies the bitterest, a government the most exact and mighty the world has seen, are its witnesses. Christ died on that cross. Christ was buried in that tomb.

But that tomb could not hold him. That death could not maintain its manacles. The morning of the first day of the week is breaking. He rises. Death has had dominion, but death has now no more dominion over him. He rises an utter and easy victor. There is no hurry. There is no evidence of strain, of struggle, and of conquest. The shroud in which they wrapped him is neatly folded and laid away. The napkin with which they had bound his head lies also in its special place. Calmly he is victor. And soon the news goes forth to his disciples, changing their sorrow into joy—changing our sorrow too, when death wraps itself about our own dead; giving us the oil of joy for mourning, the garments of praise for the spirit of heaviness. He is risen! He is risen!

This, then, is the revelation which the fact brings—that the grave is not the end, as the dog thought it, as the old pagan and much of our modern thinking bewails it; but that the grave is only a passage; that it opens lifeward on its thither side; for Christ "hath brought life and immortality to light."

THE END.

www.ingramcontent.com/pod-product-compliance
Lightning Source LLC
Chambersburg PA
CBHW032133230426
43672CB00011B/2315